The
Education
of Little Me

A Short Memoir of Connecting
Passion with Purpose

Nancy Hilliard Joyce

Printed in the United States of America

FIRST EDITION

ISBN-10: 1544027702

ISBN-13: 978-1544027708

DEDICATION

For my children, Claudia and James:

Even if you are the only people who ever read this book, it will have served its purpose. I will always love you just as God has designed you; you are the greatest gifts on Earth to me. I feel blessed that I was given the opportunity to raise you both to the best of my ability, just as my parents raised me to the best of their abilities. Always believe in yourselves and be guided by your hearts.

Love you more,

Mom

The Education of Little Me

A Short Memoir of Connecting Passion with Purpose

INTRODUCTION

On February 9th, 2017, I dragged myself out of our rented 3-story, walk-up apartment to go and hear Julie Lythcott-Haims speak at our children's school. Julie is a New York Times bestselling author of *How to Raise an Adult: Break Free of the Over-Parenting Trap and Prepare Your Kid for Success.* It was a necessary and integral time in my life as I found myself in a conundrum with our 9-year old son, who was just told he might not be a good "academic fit" for the school we had recently moved our kids to 6 months prior. I was in the process of having him re-tested but the days were collapsing in on me, just as I felt the walls of our small apartment complex were suffocating my creativity. We were new to town, and I didn't have the resources and networks that I did in Asheville, NC. That night, as I sat in the auditorium at our children's school, I felt as if Julie were speaking directly to and through me. I immediately could see a direct parallel between my own educational experiences and my son's hurdles in school. I could clearly see my parents' efforts to somehow and unknowingly instill self-efficacy in me. I immediately began wrestling with the idea of writing this book that same night.

The Education of Little Me is not just for my children. This book is also meant for parents who are struggling with allowing their children to foster their dreams while still driving them to "make a living." It is a delicate balance that fortunately my parents successfully navigated. Pouring all of their resources, which began with nothing, into me, to make me not just an "artist," but rather an artist with purpose, integrity, and grit. We are told to "follow our dreams" because ultimately, that is what will make us successful. But, will following our dreams *always* lead to "success"? What about those people who dream of making a living from gardening, ballet, art or cooking? Maybe. Maybe if we want something enough, we are willing to make the initial sacrifices, persevere throughout our struggle, and then, we too can succeed. But, does it have to be black or white?

In the pages that follow, I do not claim that the way my parents raised me is the right way to raise your child and I do not think that you have to raise your children as I was raised in order for them to be able to live out their dreams. But, what I do hope is that your children will feel both accepted by society and genuinely fulfilled when they are older. I hope they will see that you have helped steer them towards their passion without being left to the winds of social influence that can push them into inauthentic or purposeless directions. Our world is so painfully competitive that it has the potential to drown the creative ones. Our environments can darken our spirits and make us something that we were not meant to be. The secret is to find and hold onto the talents that we were born with and help to foster and unfold them in unlikely ways. Ways in which we, as children, may not have walked without the careful but weightless hand of parental guidance.

The paradox is that I am grappling with a child, not too unlike my younger self, that has more innate creativity than potential academic grit. As I write this book, I am raising my son and helping him to find a balance between his extreme imagination and his ultimate potential. Walking the line, I do not want him to lose either of these notions while aiming to give him the best of both worlds — helping him turn his potential passion into purpose is my ultimate hope.

As a visual artist who now paints for a living, I know I am in the fortunate minority. And, as much as I strive to foster our son's creativity, I lean more towards inspiring him to find a love for learning, both alternatively and conventionally, just as my parents did with me. Without wanting to put too much emphasis on either type, I am walking a tightrope with prayer, vigilance, tutoring and ultimate freedom. This sort of parenting is nothing short of painful bliss.

CONTENTS

Dearest James,

You've asked me time and time again, "Why don't you paint a painting of me?"

I told you that someday I would, and you said, "You've already painted three different paintings of Claudia."

I thought to myself that it was completely unfair of me to have done so because I usually painted girls and not boys.

"When will you paint one for me?"

"I will do it very soon," I told you.

Well, this book is not a painting, I know. But, it is a carefully written story about my struggles throughout my education. The more my story came to unfold, the more I could see you in me. As painful as some of my endeavors throughout the traditional school system were for me, they made me who I am today. I want you to remember that through everything, we are just doing what we think is right for you and Claudia. I am sure I have made and will continue to make mistakes as a parent, but please know that we have done and will continue to implement the best practices we know how to help you become the most well-rounded individual possible.

We are proud of who you are becoming and of your hard work and progress towards reaching your true potential.

The rest is up to you.

So...get after it.

And still, I promise to paint a painting of you, one day soon.

I love you,

Mom

The Education of Little Me

A Short Memoir of Connecting Passion with Purpose

Chapter 1
BELLS ON MY SHOES

"A lot of what is most beautiful
about the world arises from struggle."
- Malcolm Gladwell

Mom would drop me off at the Lewis Village apartments where Eunice lived because we couldn't afford a babysitter and I was still too young for school. Eunice would watch me free of charge. My parents met Eunice and her husband, Louie, when they lived in the Lewis Village apartments during the late '60s. Their only child, Dorothy, passed away in a tragic accident when she was just twenty-one years old, so Eunice took our family in as if we were her own. She was the closest thing that I can remember to anyone looking like Lucille Ball. Eunice was only in her mid-fifties when she first came into my life, but I remember thinking that she was older than the hills. Her personality was as wild as her short, curly, strawberry blonde hair. Each ringlet was a shiny melon color that would sometimes catch the sunlight and mesmerize me like the flames of a fire. It was thin. I could see her scalp if I looked carefully enough, it was pale, and she seemed delicate. I remember a styled platinum wig sitting on a plastic mannequin head she had in her bedroom which faced her vanity mirror. The reflection of the wig in the mirror fascinated me, but I didn't understand why she'd ever want to cover up her beautiful strawberry curls. I never recalled her actually wearing the wig, and I assumed she must have been saving it for a special occasion that didn't involve me.

Most of the time, Eunice would sit me down on her bare linoleum floor in front of *As the World Turns* or *Days of Our Lives*. I remember watching the black and white globe slowly turn like I was being hypnotized and the announcer's deep voice saying "*And now, for the next three minutes as the world turns, brought to you today by Ivory Soap, 99.44/100% Pure. It floats!*" I loved those three minutes just watching the world turn. Eunice would fold laundry and clean her apartment and then we'd have lunch together. Sometimes, we'd take long walks around the building complex picking dandelions and making wishes. She would squat down with me outside on the warm concrete paths, and we would study the ant colonies as they made their way to and from scavenges. On my favorite days, Eunice would turn my head towards the sun, rhythmically walk her fingers across my skin, and count every other freckle on my face, as if I were the most beautiful person she'd ever seen.

Louie wasn't normally at the apartment when I was dropped off. He was a train conductor. But, sometimes, Eunice would let me stand in the front seat of her powder blue Ford Mustang Cobra, and we'd drive to see Louie at the train station. Eunice loved me so much that she eventually became a third grandmother to me. Eunice would come to our house sometimes as well, to hang out with my mom in the garden or to watch my older sister and me.

According to my mother, the only day I have ever been on time was January 31st, 1972. I was a solid 9lb. 2oz. newborn baby and "squished" upon landing into the arms of my delighted mother. My older sister, Kathryn, was four years my senior and I imagine weighed nearly the same as me at the time of my arrival. She had a slight and delicate frame which would follow her into adulthood. I, on the other hand, robust and awkward, bounced into the world with a dominating presence.

Eventually, I grew a head of thick, auburn hair and paired it with a face full of freckles to match. My ever loving and carefree spirit followed me wherever I walked. And walking, well, that is a story in and of itself. My feet, like those of Forrest Gump or "Mumble" in Happy Feet, were ostensibly leading themselves into two different directions. With this discovery, in 1974, I was given a shiny pair of metal leg braces which I wore for about four months of my life. These braces, I am told, were as a follow up to

the casts that were placed on each of my legs the previous year.

Shortly after my leg braces were removed in

The metal rods spanned the length of each leg
and there at the bottom, sat a special little pair of
plastic, white, medical-looking shoes with accompa-
nying jingle bells on each foot. I really don't remember the true purpose of the small silver bells, but
mother says they "*just brought a little joy into each*

of my steps." In the end, it wasn't too damaging to my ego, as I continued to be a carefree and blithe child throughout my pre-Kindergarten years. Shortly thereafter, I set off running and didn't bother to look back.

Chapter 2
BLINDFOLDED

"You have power over your mind, not outside events.
Realize this, and you will find strength."
- Marcus Aurelius

I was oblivious to almost everything when I was in elementary school. My childhood consisted of playing with my next door neighbor, Will, and building forts inside of our large, nearly hollowed out Magnolia tree which enveloped what seemed like most of our front yard. Nothing sidelined us from our creativity. Our schemes included digging to China, catching tadpoles across the street in the creek down the hill near Julie Gray's house, roller skating in our concrete driveway, jumping from the garage roof with sheets tied together resembling small parachutes, walking to Kirsten's house in hopes of

Me and Will on his Big Wheel - 1978

raiding her snack cabinet and swimming in our cement "rock" pool which was filled with earthworms.

My sister, Kathryn, remained ahead of her time: cool and unscathed by life from my perspective. She, like most older sisters, delighted in my awkwardness but was annoyed by my presence. I never quite caught onto the fact that whenever she showed interest in playing with me, there was always a twist of events involved. She would lure me into her sphere by asking me to play games with her such as "let me blindfold you and spin you into a circle three times." During this particular activity, I remember I was wearing my favorite burnt orange t-shirt that was decorated very simply with a yellow giraffe on the front. The giraffe was tactile and was made from an ink puffy pen so that you could feel and see the texture of its spots. I was wearing matching knock-off IZOD, burnt orange short-shorts with my favorite shirt and felt rather spectacular.

She escorted me up to the top of our yard beside the creepy, old shuffleboard court that had a hand-built, outdoor fireplace at the far end of it. After the 3rd spin, she asked me to sit down on the grass. She lifted my bandana and ran off back into the house. At this moment, I realized that she had carefully sat me down on a giant pile of dog poop. This only happened once because, although naïve, I did learn from my mistakes — kind of.

There were other stories, of course, which included things like my sister entering me into a private contest with her, where I was instructed to "find the first penny" so I could be granted 'this or that' if I found it and picked it up. The penny, which I eventually found, had been recently superglued to the wooden steps in her bedroom. In the end, I would always process the fact that I was the butt of the joke rather than part of the fun.

Or the time I wanted to join her "bike club" that she and Ann Traxler, our other neighbor, had created together. The problem was that I didn't know *how* to ride a bike. So, the determined little redhead that I was, set out to ride a two-wheeled bike in order to be granted admission into this exclusive club. Every single day, from morning until dusk, Will and I would practice together on the shallow sloped grass hill in Ann's front yard. Several weeks later, I approached my sister and Ann to proudly announce that I could finally join their club. Like a bad movie ending, I was greeted with the news that the bike club had officially dissolved.

Innocent stories, many of them really nothing out of the ordinary for siblings, but served as constant reminders to both my family and me that I was one of those kids that had tunnel vision and trusting ways, which wouldn't necessarily bestow upon me the competitive mindset that I needed to be "successful" in life.

Chapter 3
THE CURTAINS CLOSED

"Try to realize it's all within yourself no one else can make you change, and to see you're only very small and life flows on within you and without you"
- George Harrison

The swim team was perfect for me; it saved me from my social drowning. It allowed me to blend with the rest of the kids. We all wore kelly green Speedo bathing suits and I was, by default, finally part of a homogenized group. The preparatory part of the meets was my absolute favorite. There was a tradition where the swimmers would load up with sugar before each race to get their heart-rates up, like that of a horse about to leave his gate. Parents in every household provided individual boxes of dry, artificially flavored Jell-O mix to their little swimmers.

We would ceremoniously dip our dirty, tongue-licked fingers into the boxes like a Wonka Fun Dip without the bother of the chalky sticks. I fondly remember the stains of red or blue dye that remained on my lips and fingertips for several days after our meets. It was like a badge of honor; I felt included!

I loved swimming because it was relaxing. At the time, I didn't have a competitive bone in my body. I would swim for the crowd and the cheers, I would swim for the dry Jell-O, and I would, most of the time, stop, mid-lane, in the deep end, to wave and smile at the parents standing around the pool screaming for their kids to swim faster. I was easy-going. I didn't care or even notice that I was coming in dead last in every single event.

During the school days, I tap-danced. My first part in an organized recital was that of a skunk. I thought it was perfect and awesome. I felt graceful and alive at the youthful age of eight. Though, my real attraction to tap dancing was with a boy named Hayes. I think Hayes was forced to dance because his mother was the instructor and she didn't have

Me (tap dancing skunk) & Kathryn.

anywhere else to take him after school. That wasn't of concern to me. Hayes had one beautiful, clear blue eye and his other eye was a deep chocolate brown. Not only was Hayes the token boy in the entire dance academy, but he was also as fascinating to me as a Siberian Husky. I gravitated towards people with unique differences; it made me feel comfortable.

By the time I was nine years old, I had started to become an actress, or so I imagined. In my first play, I was cast as a fairy in *A Midsummer Night's Dream*. I felt alive and important on the stage surrounded by many other fairies. By the age of ten, I was cast as the "Grandmother" in *Barnum & Bailey Circus Show*. It really didn't occur to me at the time that I may have gotten a speaking part because my mother was the President of the PTA. I was on my way to the big stage!

I continued with theater, and my last and final role was at the age of eleven at the Greenville Little Theater. I was given the distinctive part of one of two zebras in *Noah's Arc*. My costume resembled that of a full zip-up onesie with a clip-on tail, and I was required to walk in unison with the other zebra off the arc. This gracefully concluded my acting career, and the curtains finally closed on this chapter of my fleeting passion.

Chapter 4
WOOD AND DIRT

*"Nothing is art if it does
not come from nature."*
- Antoni Gaudi

Pine and cedar carvings from duck decoys were lined up above curled shavings of wood that lay scattered on the floor in our basement. On weekends we could sometimes find Dad downstairs among his carving tools, usually with bandages wrapped around his fingers and enthralled with detailing his handmade wooden decoys. I would sit on the dusty, chilled concrete floor in the dim light and watch him for hours as if it was the most fascinating thing on Earth.

If we begged and he was in an exceptionally

good mood, Dad would give Kathryn and me new bars of Irish Spring soap and one of his dull Swiss Army pocket knives and show us how to create our own little miniature figures. He patiently explained to us how to start with a two-dimensional sketch of a figure on the broad side of the bar and slowly chisel away at the pieces to create a three-dimensional object. This helped pass the time on rainy days and relaxed me in ways that I didn't fully understand.

Outside, my mother would plant rows and rows of flowers in her garden that sat up on our hill above the big magnolia tree. She was a gardener at heart, just like her father. She'd take railroad ties from lumber yards and set the stage for her creations. The ties acted as outlines to her forms as if they were lines in a coloring book. She would divide her tomatoes from her annuals. The colors would drip together in rows creating undulating lines like that of paint on a canvas. This was her palette.

My mom was a feminine tomboy. She didn't mind getting level with the Earth and having soil packed underneath her fingernails. Her hair, short and curly and her facial features delicate and pure. Neighbors would stop by and ask her questions about her harvest. She would share vegetables with friends and pick flowers for the PTA or anyone who needed something to brighten their day. It was second nature to her; gardening was her meditation.

Mom also had her way with the camera. She adopted a particular style that seemed pioneering for the '70s where she would take macrophotographs of children's faces that made other parents swoon. She would take portraits of the neighborhood children, develop them in her homemade darkroom, and give these invaluable gifts to parents. There was a particular light and color that ran throughout her work, usually pastel and slightly overexposed in a way that made each subject look ethereal. She rarely used a flash, and all of her work was done in natural light with faded or blurred backgrounds. She loved color. The eyes…the children's eyes were her subject matter and she wanted a relaxed look; candid and not posed. This was her trademark style.

Chapter 5
THE THREE-LEGGED ACTUARY

*"Love is a canvas furnished by nature
and embroidered by imagination."*
- Voltaire

My parents had a close-knit group of friends that would happily pack up their family-friendly Ford Country Squires and Jeep Wagoneers as soon as the weekend rolled around. I see now that my parents were young adults in their mid-thirties. However, from my perspective at that time, they were way too old to be going into the woods and sleeping inside tents for several days in a row, much less, dragging me along with them.

These camping trips took place at least four times a year from about 1977 until 1983. Mom and Dad were close friends with about five or six other couples that enjoyed the woods and outdoors as much as they did. A few times in the spring and again in the fall, we would drive from Greenville, SC to Wolf Mountain, nestled quietly within the Blue Ridge Mountains. We'd caravan with the other families, and kids of all ages would load into their

respective cars and sit amongst piles of sleeping bags, camping stoves, tents, shovels, camping food, pots, pans, etc. In the summertime, we'd head to a cabin in the woods surrounded by 17 acres of land. The land was mostly uninhabited except for a small vacant wooden cabin that sat on a tiny pond (that the parents called a lake) and two brothers who lived in a house a few miles down from the cabin.

Herbert and Herman Nicholson were the caretakers of the land. They both lived and farmed on the mountain all year round. Their accents were as pure and deep as any Appalachia native, and they always seemed to be in overalls standing at the end of the driveway as we pulled up to say hello. And, as if that weren't peculiar enough, they had a dog that they loved named Actuary. Actuary had only three legs and was given his name because, as the brothers would joke, he "put down 3 and carried 1." It was a math joke that I didn't completely understand for many years. Actuary was a good dog, and frankly, I don't think he needed a fourth leg — he darted through the trails just fine.

The dilapidated cabin came with an old wood burning stove, two rocking chairs that were always filled with cobwebs and six bunk beds. The bathroom was a hole my father had dug with his shovel behind the cabin in the woods, and there was a small natural spring that provided a constant flow of ice cold water to cook and clean with about 15 yards from the cabin. Each night, I would cover my head with my sleeping bag and assure myself that the mice couldn't get up to my top bunk.

I always knew better than to complain about the outdoor experience. I could feel that my Dad was proud of that place and wanted us to build memories to last a lifetime. The more years we clocked in the woods, the more I grew to love nature. The more I grew to enjoy nature, the tougher I became and the more connected I felt to the world around me. I recently learned that Herman has since passed away and is buried behind the cabin. I can only wonder who owns that land today and whether or not there are still weekend visitors to that area. The memories I have of the place may be all that remains — except

Me and Kathryn, Learning to love "nature".

for maybe Herman's ghost.

The November and early December camping trips carried a distinct chill with them. These particular weekend excursions were centered around entertaining the kids and cutting down Christmas trees from rows of Balsam Fir that we'd then strap to the tops of our cars and drive back down to our homes in South Carolina. The laughter was as strong as the smell of campfire smoke that drifted into the star-filled evenings. Both parents and children would put on skits for all to enjoy, tell ghost stories, roast s'mores and plan day hikes for the following morning. As much as I was lost in the woods, I felt a deep connection to those families and to my parents. I felt safe amongst the trees and within nature. Both the water and the air were clean and pure. The pull into the mountains became greater for me each passing year, and sooner than later it started to feel like home.

Chapter 6
SOUTHERN ROOTS

*"The best inheritance a parent can give
to his children is a few minutes
of their time each day."*
- M. Grundler

Anderson, South Carolina may be the first place where I was old enough to distinguish the individual sounds of both the Southern chorus frog and the Carolina locust. Since my parents grew up in Anderson, this was also where we would visit "Anna and Pops" on Dad's side and "KK and Granddaddy" on Mom's side. The Hilliard's and the Prevost's came from different parts of town. However, consistent throughout the two homes, was the loyal and steadfast love we received from them.

From my naïve and youthful perspective, Anna

and Pop's home reminded me of the Tara House in *Gone with the Wind*. It was a white, Victorian home with hunter green shutters and a wraparound porch that sat along a deserted road with pigs, donkeys, and cattle grazing in the distance. A long-roped, handmade, wooden swing hung from an old oak tree. This was the deep countryside of South Carolina, and the house was at least 100 years old and may or may not have been updated since it was first built. There wasn't anyone around to help with the house and no sign of horses or carriages, but Pops did have a really awesome pick-up truck.

Kathryn and I would play in the backyard for what felt like hours at a time. Pops, who smelled of old tobacco pipe smoke and wore faded suspenders, would whistle like a bird and call out to the Northern bobwhites that were singing in his yard. Anna was always in the kitchen frying up something with Crisco and bacon fat. That house was so rich with fascinating scents that they soaked into an everlasting area of my memory.

Deep in the back of the yard, Anna and Pops

kept some pigs that I didn't pay much attention to at the time. I had no idea they may have provided the family with an occasional meal nor did I stop to ponder their significance. What I did notice were loads of ornate chorus frogs that were only an inch or so in size that fit comfortably into each of my tiny hands. The frogs ranged in color from green to gray, with some being slight reddish-brown. They had a distinguishable black mask-like stripe across their eyes like that of Robin's leather superhero mask. These frogs led to hours of entertainment for Kathryn and me.

Inside, along the main front hallway, sat a full, commercial-size, deep freezer floor cooler. I had no idea what was kept in 95% of that cooler but can only imagine now that it was mostly filled with bacon and ham. On the top, left-side portion, however, was an ample supply of old-school Fla-Vor-Ice popsicles that we were allowed to eat if we finished our meals and stayed out of trouble.

When it was raining, or the sun was too blistering hot, Anna would set up the wooden Lincoln

Logs in the formal dining room for me to play. There, on the floor, I would build houses for hours at a time. Sometimes, she would sit with me and build, but most of the time she was in the kitchen making gravy for our biscuits and ham.

On very special occasions, Pops would pile us up into the back of his pick-up truck with a stray dog or two and drive us down the road to Jake's Candy Store. I'm not exactly sure if it was actually named "Jake's" but I know that an old man named Jake owned the place — so that's what we called it. If you can imagine what an Old Mast General store looked like in 1978, minus the apparel, clean surroundings and halogen lighting, you may be able to understand the authenticity of this place. There were buckets lined up against the walls filled with all sorts of candy. There were tobacco cigarettes on display directly next to the candy cigarettes for the kids, hard boiled eggs in large glass jars of vinegar sitting next to another large jar filled with a two-headed snake, Mexican jumping beans in small plastic cases, wooden Jacob's ladders, yo-yos, and slinkys. I'd always seem to leave with some Mary Janes or Peanut Butter Logs since they were my favorite, but I would sometimes get the Necco Wafers because those were my Mom's favorite and I wanted to share.

If we stayed with Anna and Pops while the County Fair was in town, we'd get to ride the old Farris wheel or throw some darts while we ate cotton candy. This was both rare and significant and depended on whether or not Mom and Dad lined up our visits with the fairground schedule. It was the height of all things awesome and looked a little like a scene out of *Charlotte's Web*.

KK and Granddaddy's house was a different experience altogether. We would usually visit both grandparents since they were in the same town but not stay too long at KK and Granddaddy's house. Granddaddy was a physician, and little kids were both loud and messy. Each time we came over, he'd line us up next to the sofa and check our tiny ears to see if there was any fluid in them. He had the classic professional, rugged doctor's bag with the silver

hinge and push key lock. It was a free pediatrician check-up, which was a huge bonus for Mom and Dad. Granddaddy always said we looked healthy. If we told him that we felt sick, he'd say we just needed a glass of water, some fresh air and then send us outside to play.

Granddaddy was also a gardener and a winemaker. He harvested rows and rows of grapes in his side yard and had a small outdoor shed which acted as his dispensary for bottling and labeling. He was the modern-day Renaissance man with a thick head of distinguished, wavy silver hair that was swept to the side. He'd usually escape outdoors onto one of his tractors after KK made him check our ears and noses. He was a grumpy old man most of the time, but we loved him for it, and it really didn't bother us too much.

KK had a divine spirit. She was delicate, graceful and poised. She was an avid bird watcher and paid close attention to detail. She taught us the histories of our relatives and showed us photographs of her ancestors and would never let us forget that she was born and raised in Pennsylvania. She continually reinforced manners and politeness as well as discipline and structure. We only ate off of her fine china and with her sterling silver stemware. And, although their home was a humble, one-story brick ranch house set amongst the landscape of granddaddy's corn fields, it felt distinguished.

There were rows of 16-inch Porcelain dolls, the kind with eyes that closed when you laid them flat. They all wore colorful, fancy Victorian dresses and were lined up against the side wall of the guest room. We weren't allowed to play with them; they ere only allowed to stare at us when we were trying to sleep at night. Sometimes, against KK's wishes, I would lay them on their backs at night so that I couldn't see the whites of their eyes.

KK took pleasure in treating us like dolls as well. She didn't like my hair to be wispy or out of place so she would use something called Dippity-do which was a thick, goopy, dark lime green gel inside of a clear, plastic container. KK would use a comb to slick back my hair with the Dippity-do and secure it firmly with bobby pins on each side so that she could "see my pretty face." Honestly, I never felt very pretty at all when I saw myself in the mirror afterward.

KK adapted to South Carolina like she was a native. She owned an original Lite-Brite set and had endless amounts of paper dolls for us to dress. She relished in reading stories aloud to us from *The Little Women* series and she'd refer to me as Laura Ingalls. She served us poached eggs from porcelain egg cups and nurtured stray cats in the wooded area behind her home.

Anderson was a place of comfort for me. It was filled with my parent's family who always made me feel unique as they continually encouraged my creative ways. I never felt anything but welcome there, no matter how I looked or dressed. I believe this was the foundational inclusion and nonjudgmental part of my life that ultimately gave me the self-esteem and confidence I would unknowingly need later in life when things began to feel less controlled and safe for me.

Chapter 7
WHEN TIME STOOD STILL

"It may be hard for an egg to turn into a bird: it would be a jolly sight harder for it to learn to fly while remaining an egg. We are like eggs at present. And you cannot go on indefinitely being just an ordinary, decent egg. We must be hatched or go bad."
- C. S. Lewis

It was midsummer and I was heading into middle school soon. Mom had arranged for me to attend Camp Gwynn Valley for several weeks in July. She was visibly sick and seemed pre-occupied with her own life, but I was too young to suspect anything was wrong with her. Every summer before this one, she'd been a counselor at the camp, but this summer was different. She told me that she had other things to do at home while I went to camp. Luckily, I knew the ropes and felt relatively confident about the arrangement. I was dropped off without a hitch, but towards the end of my session, I received a handwritten postcard from my mother.

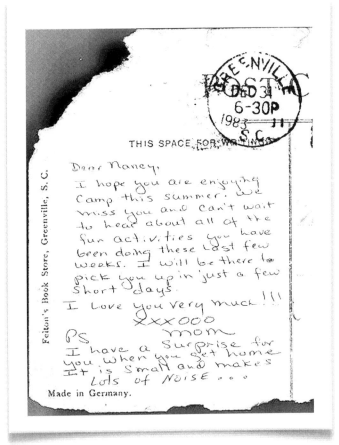

I had never wished for a trumpet or any sort of small instrument. I wondered if the surprise was a puppy or a hamster. My imagination ran wild! The last few nights, I would lie awake in my bunkbed at camp and think about all the endless things this surprise could possibly be. I had always prayed for a little sister but knew this wasn't a possibility. Anyway, I was eleven years old by now and had been the youngest child in the family for my entire life. I quickly buried that ridiculous idea.

Contrary to my mind games on the ride home from camp, Mom revealed to me that she was pregnant. It was a very tricky conversation that consisted of me staring out of the car window for most of the ride back down the mountain. I was relatively confident that it was my doing — from my prayers and all — and wondered if it was a good thing or a bad thing that I had done. Although, there is one particular thing I understood immediately — I would soon, at the age of twelve, become the middle child.

My dad was working steadily as a corporate lawyer at a Life Insurance Company and circumstantially, as the family was growing, we found a larger home. Kathryn was now fifteen and entering into high school. She stayed in the public school system because she fit in there. She was dynamic, gorgeous, strong-willed, daring and tough. I was still a bit shy, awkward and trying to fit into my own skin. I think my parents were afraid I would drown in the public school system. After all, I was seemingly lost most of the time anyway.

The *big* switch from public to private school was a massive leap of faith financially and geographically for our family. This transition came to us complete with all the socioeconomic trappings as well as plenty of academic red tape and measurements. Everything changed. I used to have the freedom to ride my bike for several miles to and from school with the other neighborhood kids. These unknowing parallel implications of biking to school and back would eventually impact my future. But for now, I wasn't thinking in metaphors. I only understood two things. Not only was I much farther from my new school, but also, it was no longer "cool" to ride my bike. After all, this was middle school.

Against the sneers of peer pressure, I kept riding

my bike. I also continued to swim on the swim team and started jogging with my dad on the weekends. I was relatively fit for a girl my age and felt ready for a challenge. I was slowly discovering that taking calculated risks made my heart beat in a more rhythmic way. About this time, I also discovered that there was a triathlon in the area. It consisted of a 1/2-mile swim in open lake waters, an 11-mile road bike stretch and concluded in a 10k run. With my parent's help, I registered for the triathlon with very little knowledge of the competitive intensity of the race.

The lake swim became tumultuous and aggressive as I kicked and had little vision ahead of me in the dark waters. There was no room to breathe, and adults of all ages swam alongside me, unknowingly batting my face and swatting my legs. I ran out of the concrete boat dock at the end of the swim and stubbed the big toe on my left foot so severely that blood soaked through my sock and sneaker as I was peddling the eleven miles. The run was tough, but I

1984 South Carolina Triathlon

had the adrenaline of a pre-teen. Among nearly three hundred participants, I think I came in second to last, just barely outrunning a man who looked to be in his early eighties. I was proud of myself for just finishing the race.

My little sister arrived on March 15th, 1984. She was named after Dad. At this moment, my life forever changed again. For quite some time I honestly wondered if I had brought her into existence with my own sheer will, but I also believed that regardless of how she arrived, she was a blessing. Glenn was *my* baby. At least that was what I liked to imagine as I dressed her up in all sorts of clothes

and posed her in different positions like she was a real, live Xavier Roberts Cabbage Patch Kid. I would push Glenn in her stroller when we would visit different places with the family, and I would pretend that other people saw me as mature enough to have given birth to her myself. She brought great joy to my life.

Glenn needed a lot of attention, as most babies do, and Kathryn was sixteen at the time and was being closely observed by both Mom and Dad. This natural preoccupation that my parents had with my sisters left me to my own devices. I remember enjoying the fact that their focus was no longer on me. I gravitated towards doing my own thing. It was around this time when I found myself sitting and drawing for several hours in a row without taking breaks.

One particular Saturday in 1984, I knelt by the glass table in the living room with a No.2 HB pencil and created a detailed drawing from a magazine that I had found of a Benetton model. In my mind, she was the most beautiful thing I had ever seen. The beaded headpiece she wore took me several hours to complete, and I relished every single moment that I spent drawing her. Time stood still, and I finally felt entirely at peace.

My first independent drawing at twelve years old

Chapter 8
LOST

"Jumping from failure to failure with undiminished enthusiasm is the big secret to success."
- Savas Dimopoulos

My parents ultimately realized just how far behind in the academic arena I was compared to the other kids my age. I had, out of sheer desperation, begun to garner my comedic skills within the classroom. At home, I tried to get as much attention as possible, but Glenn was now seven months old and required most of Mom's energy. Dad was working his tail off at work to support his three daughters. Kathryn was sixteen and was testing her independence in the public school systems.

November 5, 1984

Mrs. R. Glenn Hilliard
28 Boxwood Lane
Greenville, South Carolina 29605

Dear Mr. Hilliard:

Thank you for your visit Thursday morning, and of course I appreciate your concern for Nancy's academic progress. I do think that some of her problems stem from Nancy's intellectual immaturity—symptoms of which are her short attention span, superficial treatment of homework assignments, inefficient use of study time, and so forth. On the other hand, I do want to emphasize that Nancy's academic aptitudes are weak compared to the average student enrolled on this campus. Moreover, some verbal skills (vocabulary, reading speed and comprehension) are by independent school standards drastic in their deficiency.

For the time being, I think you should regard "C's" as highly satisfactory grades in such subjects as English and social studies—and occasional "D's" may prove unavoidable. As Nancy matures, develops motivation, and becomes a more efficient student, her grades should improve. In the meantime, school will at times be a struggle—as parental support, teacher direction, and various incentives augment the inconsistent effort of a typical middle school child whose priorities are other than academic performance.

Certainly Nancy is a delightful girl, and we very much enjoy her company at ██████ When I can be of any further assistance to you or to Nancy, please let me know. Meanwhile, many thanks again for dropping by.

With every good wish, I remain

Sincerely,

I knew I was getting behind as well and noticed that studying was truly painful and uninteresting to me. My focus was all over the place and never where they told me it should have been directed. I am sure I must have had ADD and eventually learned to accommodate myself during academic situations without diagnosis or medication. It was at this point when my parents decided they needed to meet with my new school and it was shortly after the meeting that they received the following letter from the school.

My parents were blindsided by this letter. They believed in me and knew that there was something inside of me that had yet to develop or bloom. They fought for me and worked tireless hours to keep me at that private school. Mom immediately wanted to dispose of the letter, but Dad convinced her to keep it. He argued that it might serve some sort of purpose one day. So, they filed it away for safe keeping.

Eventually, they took me to be tested at the Speech, Hearing and Learning Center to make sure they were not missing any pieces of the puzzle. The psychologists who tested me came back with reports of an excellent IQ and math scores that were well above average. Reading and writing scores, on the other hand, were extremely below average and in need of immediate intervention.

Twice a week, Mom would drop me off at the Speech, Hearing and Learning Center so that I could work on reading comprehension and proficiency. Every Saturday morning, I was relegated to my bedroom in the far corner of the house to work through the pages of a notebook called "Wordly Wise." I was required to complete one chapter each weekend and wasn't allowed to play until it was finished. I couldn't see the bigger picture at the time, all I could see was that I wanted to be free to do my

own thing. It took me about 5 minutes to discover that there was an answer key at the back of the notebook. This was very helpful.

My parents believed that I was trying my best and they were also doing everything in their powers to save me from my academic demise. Art continued to be my most enjoyable subject even though Art was not considered an academic discipline in the '80s. My grades continued to suffer, but I was slowly discovering what made me feel alive.

Chapter 9
SUMMERS TURN

"The thing that is really hard, and really amazing, is giving up on being perfect and beginning the work of becoming yourself."

- Anna Quindlen

My summers slowly began to morph into unchartered territory following the 6th-grade at private school. Gone were the days of summer camps, sleepovers and playing with my baby sister. The very first summer after middle school, I was driven by my mom from our home in South Carolina up to Virginia for six weeks of summer school. It was my opportunity to pre-take courses that would be given in 7th-grade so that I could "get ahead," as my parents put it. I knew in reality, however, that I was being driven up there so I could "keep up" with everyone else once I returned home.

I only recall one memory from that particular summer. There was a boy who actually liked me. I didn't pay much attention to him while I was there, mainly because I was trying to find my *own* way. He wrote me several letters and poems which he gave me throughout the summer, and I found them to be very heartfelt and creative. It was during the last week of camp when I realized both humanness and heartache worked on a level divided from the rest.

This boy, who liked me for reasons I never understood, was found threatening to jump off a building. The fire department and police arrived, and he was safely lowered from the roof. He handed me one last poem and was taken home later that afternoon. I couldn't believe it had anything to do with me. Guilt swelled over me, and I became confused about how anyone could ever feel this way towards another person, much less, me. I was deeply sad for him and internalized blame for his actions. I left that summer in distress.

The following summer, I was sent to New

Hampshire to a place where my older sister had gone several summers before me. I knew she had hated it because I remember her arriving home and relaying horror stories of sleeping in tents and swimming in frozen lakes. I was not looking forward to being so far away from home and knew it would be an awful experience. To my surprise, however, that was one of the best summers of my life.

It turned out I was fascinated by living in the outdoors and studying under exposed canvas pup tents. The morning chill was inspirational and made me feel full of life. I created strong bonds with the other summer school kids and received my American Red Cross Lifeguard certification in the cold New Hampshire lakes. I excelled in academics and participated in Art studio courses every single day. The talent show was memorable, and my skit won 1st place with a standing ovation. I left that summer with the Camper of the Year award and begged to return the following summer. It's a mystery how these things happened. I continued to find the unexpected in unusual places and thrived in unconventional settings. I returned the following summer at the age of fifteen.

The second time around wasn't nearly as fulfilling. I was coming out of my shell and beginning to feel independent. With this new found individualism, I took more risks and wanted to show my uniqueness to the world. In an organized event one afternoon I rode in the camp van to the closest town. This was an opportunity for campers to grab lunch outside of the isolated camp area. During this group trip, I found a hole-in-the-wall shop and went inside and asked the clerk to pierce my left ear — for a second time. I was later pulled aside by the head of school because rumors were going around that I had been smoking pot. I didn't even know what pot was at the time, so the threat was not only incredibly intimidating and embarrassing but also quite educational at the same time. Needless to say, I did not return for a third summer.

Chapter 10
POISON

"All alone! Whether you like it or not,
alone is something you'll be quite a lot!"
- Dr. Seuss

I made it to 9th-grade, but the transition for me was similar to walking through thick mud while wearing one extra large boot on only my left foot. By this time, Mom had artfully devised a carpool system for me so that I could get to school on time. His name was Bill, and he was starting his senior year in high school. I suppose my mom was friends with his mother and Bill must have needed the money to buy beer or something. I think mom paid him $10 a week to pick me up and drive me to school.

Bill would honk the horn, and most of the time,

that would be my alarm clock. Mom would yell back to me that Bill's Mustang was in the driveway waiting. I would struggle out of bed, wash my face and throw on some stupid outfit I most likely spent hours picking out the night before. By the time I got into his car, either Poison or Van Halen was blasting out of his side windows. Bill never looked at or spoke to me. He hated me, and he hated this ridiculous deal. I am sure he could have made money by just picking it out of my pocket during lunch, but I think his mom thought this was his community service effort. He'd speed to school so fast that I didn't know from day to day if we would ever live to see tomorrow. He'd park, get out and leave me in his car to fumble out alone. I would walk into school scrambled like the eggs I wished I had gotten for breakfast.

I seemed to be keeping my head above water with mostly C's and the occasional B here and there. Although I always somehow seemed to maintain an A in math, which was a solvable puzzle for me. And Art; Art was my first true love. I would count the hours until Art class each day. I had even won a few awards along the way for drawing. As an added bonus, my Art teacher, Mrs. Abrams, started to invite me to private life drawing classes with her after school so I could work on the human figure. She was eager to help me study forms, proportions, perspective, shading, and other fundamentals that go along with learning to draw. She knew that it was important for an aspiring artist to understand movement, weight, balance, and tension within a drawing. After several figure-drawing classes away from campus, I asked my mom if it was okay that I was sketching nude male and female models after school. That ended rather abruptly.

What I thought was making me into a *real* artist was actually horrifying to my parents. As much as they liked the idea that I had this creative talent, they continued to tell me that I would never be able to make a career from it. In a matter of weeks, I went back to the drawing board. I started to believe that I could become an architect. You know, work with numbers and draw house plans — like that of Frank

Lloyd Wright. It seemed attainable and interesting to me. I asked my parents if I could interview one of their architect friends.

They decided there would be no harm in it and let me hang out with Judy Cromwell at her home in Brushy Creek Farm for the day. Her yard was lush with wildflowers and perennials that climbed up old brick walls. All of my senses heightened as I swept her life with my eyes in a moment's time. She had this airy style about her that seemed so relaxed and joyful. She wore a smile that extended beyond her face, and her walk was almost like a dance, and the green surroundings of her yard, a stage. She was a collector. A collector of art, colored bottles, plants and all things fanciful. It was at that moment when I decided that architecture was my calling and this would be my career path.

Within a few months, however, Mom and Dad convinced me that architects were faced with too much competition and the profession was an impossible one to find success with unless I was extremely fortunate and determined. I suppose my lack of resolve proved them right. I ultimately concluded that if I were destined to accomplish something, I would not avert from its path.

Several months afterward, I would bring home page after page of "notes" from class with drawings of my teachers on them. This made it impossible for me to progress academically. So, in a desperate effort to save her drowning child, Mom found me an after-school tutor to fill in the gaps. I was so thankful for this help. The tutor would meet me after school and talk to me at length about history or science. Unfortunately, my tutor was my age and would eventually just complete my homework for me. I suppose that it made him feel more successful. It certainly was a time-saver for both of us.

The time finally arrived for me to get my driver's license. I was fifteen. Dad required Kathryn and me to be able to drive a stick shift before taking our driver's test. He told us that he wanted us to "be able to drive any car on the road, including an 18-wheeler" if we were ever in a situation where that was necessary. It all went down in our 1980, diesel-engined, brick red International Scout. The coordination of holding down the extended clutch with your left foot, while pressing the glow plug located to the left of the steering wheel and holding the break with your right foot, as you simultaneously started the engine, was in and of itself a complete zoo. Once the driving finally began, it was the steep hills that created the most significant challenges. The delicate balance of lifting your right foot off of the brake, while pressing the gas at the same time as you released the clutch with your left foot, just slightly enough to not roll back down the hill was enough to make you sweat. There was no room for mistakes.

Ernest Folger was our next door neighbor. He and his wife, Mary, were in their late seventies, so Mom and Dad decided Ernest was perfect for the job. He would wake me up early in the morning and hand me the keys to our Scout. We'd head out of the driveway together and up the back hill that sloped upward at a steep 60° angle. We'd practice the balance of stop and go on the hill at least fifteen times in a row. The goal was to push the gas just enough, and release the clutch in such a way, that my decline backward down the hill was slight enough to avoid the imaginary car behind us. Then, he'd direct me to The Donaldson Center in Greenville, and we'd drive around the blocked-off side roads until he was ready for lunch. We did this a few days out of each week together during the summer of 1987 until he felt I was ready for the driver's test.

There I sat in the driver's seat, next to a complete stranger, that had been given the responsibility of passing or failing me on the road test. I was already sweating from the fact that it was mid-summer in South Carolina and also because there was no air conditioning in the Scout. I was terrified as I realized that my fate lay in the hands of the DMV man to my right. Parallel parking had always been my favorite. I swooshed in and out of the small area like it was second nature. The side roads were fine as well. I didn't get nervous driving through neighborhoods where there were no other cars in sight.

Once on the main road, however, my

confidence began to wane as we waited at a red light alongside a dozen other tenured drivers. The light turned green, and I went from neutral to what I thought was 1st gear and pressed the gas. We immediately lunged forward in unison with a fast and aggressive jerk toward the windshield. Without hesitation, I tried again figuring that maybe I had not adjusted the gas fast enough while simultaneously lifting the clutch. We slammed forward again into our seat belts. I felt beads of water rapidly dripping down the Inside of my shirt and looked for assistance from my guide. He shrugged his shoulders with seeming empathy and slight fear toward our impending stall.

Horns sounded all around us, and it suddenly struck me that the man sitting to my right was clueless about operating the old Scout. In desperation, I tried two more times to get the truck moving and then — it just happened. I realized within a split second that the stick was pushing into 3rd gear, which was located immediately to the right of 1st gear, but slightly to the right and then upward. I corrected my stick and off we went. I flew through the yellow light and sped back to the DMV like I was on a police chase. I quickly wove around cars without using either of my blinkers. I knew I must have failed the test back at the light and felt no need to follow any more traffic rules. I wanted out.

I halted to an angry stop and the test administrator got out of the truck. He looked directly at me with sympathy in his eyes and said, "You really did a great job. I am sorry I couldn't help. Come back in two weeks and try again. I know you will pass." I wanted to hug him for not yelling at me or making me feel any worse about my embarrassing panic-attack on Woodruff Road. I think he knew anyone would have struggled with the old diesel stick-shift under those circumstances. And, he was right; I did pass two weeks later and was a better driver due to having failed the first time.

I joined the cheerleading squad and was beginning to excel in both swimming and track — I went from being last on the teams to many times coming in first place. My body and mind were beginning to catch up with other kids my age, and this was helpful on the athletic front. My dad would train with me for track races and frequently sprint beside me during finish line runs. The spring following my 10th-grade year, I was awarded MVP of the high school track team. I was making progress outside of the classroom, and it felt amazing. I started to develop tried and true friendships as well; both girls and boys who had known me since my elementary school days began to protect me like their sister. At the same time, I was being harassed by some of the most popular kids at the school, and the relentless teasing from some of the kids was taking a profound and irreversible toll on my self-worth.

I remember walking past a group of older, extremely popular boys in the hallway. They were all crowded around a doorway just hanging out, looking cool and having fun from my perspective. I'm not sure why I glanced their way, I suppose for approval or out of curiosity, but as soon as I did, one of the top dogs in the group looked straight at me and said, "You're as ugly as a bat." They all laughed hysterically, and I just walked off trying not to trip on my own two feet. I had always thought that this particular guy looked like Ricky Schroder, so this was especially painful for me.

Within months, the boys my age were also saying cruel things about me that lasted throughout the year. It culminated with the most popular girl in our class cornering me in the bathroom and making me pull up my brand new sleeveless, teal green, Esprit sweater to prove to her that I wasn't stuffing my bra. She told me that everyone was talking about it and that she was asked to get the proof. There was no proof. She left me standing alone in the bathroom, feeling vindicated yet mortified. I don't think I ever cried about these things. I think they just stuck with me a little too long. Longer than necessary.

I believe the straw that really broke this poor camel's back was when I was sixteen years old. I was sitting in Algebra class in an open classroom setting. The classroom walls only went up about 10 feet with a two-foot gap from the drop ceiling above us. The partial sidewalls acted as barriers from other classrooms, but with only three sides to each room. There was no door, per se, but rather an opening 1/4 the area of the room. The classrooms were at least two deep extending to the far edges of the main school wall. In the center, or the heart of these classrooms, was the library. This was where everyone went in between classes or during breaks.

Our Algebra teacher had just completed a huge problem on the chalkboard, and I noticed a mistake. I raised my hand and corrected him. He slowly reworked the problem from start to finish, and instead of being quietly humble, my mouth began to form words. Before I could think to shut myself up, I mumbled out loud, "I told you."

Let me remind you that this was 1987. In the mid-'80s, new curriculum theories were just beginning to unfold, and the teacher-student relationship was that of repression and submission. My teacher assumed his role and proceeded to scream and spit words at me that I had never heard in my life. Then, before I knew what was happening, an eraser and several pieces of chalk were being thrown towards me. He grabbed my upper arm and aggressively and quite forcefully marched me out to the library where everyone was sitting with mouths wide open. They all quickly looked down as I, red-faced and ashamed, walked slowly over to a sofa in the corner of the library.

I have no idea how I got off of that sofa or how I actually finished the day. Not too long afterward, however, there were quiet whispers at home which revolved around the theme of boarding school.

Chapter 11
REPEAT AFTER ME

"Education is the most powerful weapon
which you can use to change the world."
- Nelson Mandela

It was inevitable. I needed a change. I needed a boost. I needed to jump start my life again. Everything seemed to be moving in slow motion, and I wasn't making a solid case for myself. As much as I wanted to remain in the status quo, I knew that I was on the road to nowhere. I was determined to go somewhere, but I couldn't quite find my *True North*. The guidance I needed was in my parents. They were there for me even though I couldn't see the path that was directly in front of me.

My older sister was sent to boarding school in

Maryland for her junior and senior years in high school; she was now a freshman in college. My younger sister was barely four years old. It seemed logical and, although a significant financial sacrifice for my family, it became their first priority. They would talk about it often, but I couldn't seem to wrap my head around the idea of ever leaving home.

I still sought the protection of my parents, and I never felt as secure as Kathryn seemed to look. I couldn't imagine life any other way than the way it was right at that particular moment.

Dad started breaking me into the idea of going away to school by strategically placing brochures and pamphlets around our house. The plan still seemed downright foreign to me, so Dad announced that we were going on a road trip. We drove for days and miles at a time visiting at least seven schools up and down the East coast. It felt like I was being sent to college at the age of sixteen. I was terrified to think of starting a new life, away from home, without my family. The campuses seemed huge and overwhelming to me.

A single-sex education was the unilateral decision made for me. Apparently, it was never an option for me to go to a co-ed boarding school. It was explicit and unspoken that I didn't need the distraction of boys. They didn't pay positive attention to me anyway, and I certainly couldn't afford to focus on my hair more than my grades. This narrowed things down a bit for me when making the final decision.

In the end, the only school that felt comfortable to me and provided me with a sliver of hope was a boarding school located in a quaint, Southern Virginia town called Chatham. Chatham had a population of approximately 1,300 residents at the time with a mere span of 2 square miles. Paradoxically, the town was initially named Competition but in 1852 was changed by the Virginia General Assembly. I certainly didn't need additional competition at that time in my life, so this identity upgrade was a game changer. I can't imagine my parents ever encouraging me to apply to Competition Hall.

Chatham was situated among farmland and rolling hills. There was a Quonset Hut style movie theatre which opened in 1945 that sat about 300 yards from the school and a bright, candy apple red streetcar diner that served the best chili dogs I had ever tasted in my life. Some knew Chatham for its foray of American architecture which included representations of pre-Revolution, Federal, Victorian, and the post-Victorian era. But, most notably, Georgia O'Keeffe had graduated from Chatham Hall in 1905.

It was the summer after my sophomore year in high school, and we were at Litchfield Beach for vacation. I had recently been accepted to Chatham Hall, and I was on my way to becoming a rising junior. Or, so I thought. Mom and Dad asked me to take a walk with them on the beach just before sunset one evening. I knew that it meant they needed to talk to me about something and wanted me to be active and out of the house. The beach had always been a comforting place to me, and the waves reminded me of the moon which always seemed to give me perspective on life. Which was exactly what I needed at that time.

During this walk on the beach, my parents carefully and verbally recalled my educational days up to that point. They spoke to me about living up to my potential and career objectives. They talked about how much hope they had for my future and relayed their thoughts on setting higher goals. They peeled

apart layers of academic struggle I had me
way and pieced together objectives for
ahead. And then, without warning, they just said it.
They told me that although I had been accepted as
a junior, that they were enrolling me as a sophomore.

Time stood still, and the blood slowly sank from
my heart. I stared blankly out at the ocean and saw
waves crashing onto the sanded Earth, and my ears
began to ring. I remember telling Mom that I
thought the salt inside the waves were the tears that
God was shedding for me. I swallowed hard, but the
lump inside my throat wouldn't go down. A tingling
sensation numbed my face. I felt like such a failure.
Not only was I then scared stiff of leaving home, I
knew that I would never be able to fit in with the
girls in my class. The embarrassment was almost too
much for me to handle. The guilt of being an average to below average student nearly swallowed me
whole. I quietly turned introspective for the next few
weeks.

Chapter 12
POLYESTER BLOOMERS

"Resilience is built from real hardship
and cannot be bought or manufactured."
- Julie Lythcott-Haims

It was at Chatham Hall that my life would change forever. I arrived on campus and was assigned a roommate. I brought a couple rolled up Grateful Dead, Cat Stevens, and Crosby, Stills, Nash & Young posters that Kathryn had handed down to me. I had heard a little Cat Stevens from the boombox that she carried around in the front seat of her brown Ford Bronco and from watching *Herald and Maude* with her on VHS cassette tape but honestly couldn't have told you much about them or the Grateful Dead. I banked on the fact that she was cooler than I, so I figured I had a head start with this whole *become who you want to be* persona.

My roommate arrived with short, blonde, over-styled, shoulder-length hair and bangs that were curled half up and half down. They were then locked into place with layers of hairspray. She had bright blue eyes and a very self-assured way about her. I wore my hair straight and long and was going for the hippie vibe even though I had no business in, or knowledge of, that era. It was like Bonnie Tyler and Joan Baez sharing a room together in the '90s. She hung her Led Zeppelin, Guns N' Roses, and INXS posters above her single bed and we both figured we'd last for about a week sleeping in the same room together.

Much to my surprise, Karen quickly became not only my roommate but also one of my best friends at boarding school. We were inseparable. Eventually, she ended up throwing away all of her hairspray, but also, not too long after we were living together, she was taping a group of her own Grateful Dead posters on the wall. Sooner than later we were singing in unison to both Janis Joplin and Jerry

Garcia. Neither of us was musical at all, but we both had an extreme affinity for music that ran deep in our blood and drew us together like moths to a flame.

Chatham was good for me. It allowed me to spread my wings and become the girl I wanted to be without the worry of judgment from others. It was like a clan of young girls, all showing their true colors and finding themselves at the same time. We were part of a tribe. It felt perfect and natural to me and was just where I needed to be at the time. I also discovered that at least five of my very close friends were also repeating their sophomore year, so it soon became something we didn't think about too much. We all knew it was for the best and felt great that we were in it together.

Slacking off wasn't an option. The classes were small, ranging from only five to thirteen girls depending on the subject. The teachers were a constant part of our lives. They had a genuine interest in our paths and daily routines. Our dorm rooms were in the same building as the classrooms. If you were missing from a class, certain teachers would send another student up to knock on your door. There was a motivation and a sincere interest in learning that I had not previously experienced. Friends held you accountable, and the teachers believed in us as much as our parents and still expected 110% from us. The love of learning flowed over me, and I began to excel.

Mr. Bruning was a tall, stately, teddy bear of an English teacher who was well into his sixties. He was the first teacher to take a genuine interest in my half-structured writing; he wouldn't put up with it. Mr. Bruning was liberal with his red ballpoint pen and would write detailed notes and instructions in the margins of my essays explaining why I couldn't make up my own words. He would restructure sentences for me and pull me aside after class as if to beg me to make sense of my thoughts. The pain he showed for my explosive creativity was almost palpable. He could sense that I had something inside me that needed to get out onto paper but couldn't bear the way in which I would vomit poetic sounding iterations into my notebooks. He would stand on his broad, wooden executive-looking table, while we all sat in chairs around him, staring in awe, and he would act out scenes of a play or poem with his fake sword. He was just like Robin Williams in *Dead Poets Society*; he too incorporated ancient traditions and high standards. When the movie came out later in 1989, I was convinced Mr. Bruning was their inspiration.

Chatham Hall was divided into two intramural colors which were assigned to each student on the day of their acceptance. Upon entry, I was a designated to the gold team. Generally speaking, they appointed your roommate to the opposite color, which in this case, was purple. The colors were derived from the school flower, the Iris. Intramural sports were centered on your given school color, and you wore this color throughout your years at Chatham Hall. During the '80s, we were provided thick, unbreathable polyester kilts and bloomers to match. The gold kilts were more of a mustard "golden rod" color than a real gold, and the purple was a bright eggplant color that I hated. Together, the polyester glistened in the sun and was just about as ugly as you can imagine.

One of the first ways I began to rebel was by not wearing my matching, elastic-legged, polyester

My painting of Chatham Hall

bloomers under my kilt. I figured no one would know the difference and I had my underwear on so I didn't think it was a big deal. Ms. Wagoner was head of the athletic department at the time. She was a woman of both physical and authoritative stature. She wore her pants high, proud and around the widest part of her belly and used a golf cart to travel to the lower field as well as to each meal time. Ms. Wagoner had a very thick German accent that she used quite liberally to scare the crap out of us. She had a whistle hanging around her neck both day and night. I loved her.

Ms. Wagoner didn't mess around. She was someone who not only intimidated me, but I also admired and adored her. She was my Margaret Thatcher. She would lift my kilt unexpectedly, as Ivan Pavlov conditioned his dog, when I least expected it and catch me without my bloomers. She'd blow that whistle so loud that the neighboring towns could hear and she'd yell with her accent, "Run! Go Nancy run…noooow!!!" I'd have to run the perimeter of the field until she realized that, like Forrest Gump, I loved running and wasn't suffering in the least. Eventually, she'd conclude that she needed me more on the actual field than on the sidelines. I think every so often I would purposely forget to wear my bloomers just to get a rise out of her or perhaps to get the attention I was missing from my parents on a daily basis.

Chapter 13
THE GOVERNOR'S SCHOOL

"Nothing you do for children is ever wasted.
They seem not to notice us, hovering, averting
our eyes, and they seldom offer thanks,
but what we do for them is never wasted."
- Garrison Keillor

By this time, it was fairly obvious to both my parents and my teachers that I had a deep fascination with the Arts. At this same juncture, an opportunity arose for me to apply to the Summer Program at the Governor's School for the Arts located back in Greenville, SC. I felt strongly about pursuing this venture and took every moment possible to align myself with the tools I needed for this to happen.

I pulled a portfolio together of my drawings and paintings. The requirements were strenuous, and the Governor's School was looking for a broad range of talent. Some of the work, I already had, and it was a natural addition to my selected pieces of art, but other prerequisites had me working overtime to make sure I met and surpassed their standards. After several months, I was finally ready to send in my application and shortly thereafter, I was accepted to attend the 6-week summer residential program before heading into my junior year at Chatham Hall.

The orientation was fast. There was no time to waste. The professors and instructors gave us a tour of the visual arts building, and we quickly got down to business. It was the first time in my artistic life that I realized just how average I was compared to the rest of the population. I was thrown into a situation where my "talent" looked more like a mere fascination. I was all of a sudden surrounded by superb young, emerging artists from across South Carolina ranging from fifteen to eighteen years old.

It was an incredibly humbling, awe-inspiring and enriching summer for me. It gave me infinite hope for what was possible to create in an artistic world. I learned the technical aspects of perspective as well as being forced to paint and draw several self-portraits. Never in my seventeen years had I studied the structure of my face so intently; an odd yet poignant thing for a teenager who was trying to find her way.

The foundational groundwork of the Governor's School for the Arts was unknown to me at the time. I couldn't process the effects it would have on me years down the road, but looking back, I see now this was an opening in a dark place for me. A wellspring in the depths of a canyon that I was looking to explore. Back on top of that mountain, in the traditional school system, I was scrambling to be fulfilled. It was an insatiable path for the creative mind and no matter which direction I would turn, I felt clouded. That summer was, and remains to be, one of the most profound growth periods of my life as an artist.

Chapter 14
LIGHT A CANDLE

"Don't be pushed by your problems.
Be led by your dreams."
- Ralph Waldo Emerson

It was 1989 and the beginning of my junior year at Chatham Hall. We were informed that a category 5 storm named Hurricane Hugo was ready to rip up the Southeastern shoreline. Our dorm moms had us huddle in the hallways together, and we talked about the possibility of our school being damaged by the winds and rain. I wasn't worried about it coming up to Virginia though, Ms. LaDuke (whom we called "La") was listening to the weather radio and kept me in close contact with what was happening in South Carolina. I was worried about my parents in the up-state as well as Granddaddy and KK's inlet house on the coast of South Carolina. This was one of the first times I found myself to be incredibly homesick and it was La who could sense that I was an emotional wreck. She did everything in her power to keep me calm and distracted.

The storm crept into the later hours of the night, and we slowly fell to sleep leaning on one another against our piles of pillows and blankets inside the hallways. When the sun rose the next morning, I contacted my parents and learned that KK and Granddaddy's inlet house had been virtually flattened. Luckily, my family was safe, and the inlet home was eventually reconstructed to match its previous 1970's décor. At the same time, however, there was a different kind of hurricane brewing inside our home. In an unexpected turn of events, my parents informed me that they were moving to Colorado because Dad had been hired to work out of Denver. The realization that they would no longer be a simple car ride away made me feel more imbalanced than anything I could ever imagine.

The only phones we had access to were located

in the basement of each building. The coin-operated pay phones were lined up in groups of three, but there were always several girls at any given moment waiting in line to call their boyfriends or parents. With this limited access, I rarely spoke to Mom and Dad, and when I did, it was brief and one-sided. Mom was strategic when asking me questions thus diverting the attention away from herself.

Because of this distance, it was close to six months into the sickness when I discovered Dad had contracted a severe case of Lyme Disease. Apparently, the advanced stages of the disease had dramatically taken a toll on Dad's body, and it was not until he was coming into the clear and healing that I found out about the full effect it had taken on him. The severity of the situation led my parents to side-step this reality for me. Their protective instinct was always to shield me from unnecessary worry.

I began to do the same with them, perhaps in an unconscious way. I would only call with good news about sports or academics. The rest of the stuff I would lay on my girlfriends. The smokehouse was a place of refuge for over 50% of the girls at Chatham. You had to get smoking permission from your parents to go inside the 9' x 9' x 9' outdoor brick structure, but no faculty ever manned the area, so it became a sort of free-for-all outhouse where we could go after each meal or sport in order to vent. There was a five-foot brick wall that faced the opening of the smokehouse that supposedly acted as a shield for visitors, so they didn't have to see all the teenage girls smoking cigarettes. I usually perched up on top of the wall because I wasn't a smoker and didn't have written permission to be there. I loved most everyone inside of the smokehouse though, and it was within those walls that I took my first drag of a cigarette. I wanted to become a real smoker so badly and tried several times to make it a thing for myself, but it always made me feel nauseous. Luckily, it just never caught on with me.

My obsession with fire became an entirely different story once I joined the group of acolytes at St. Mary's Chapel. The small Episcopal chapel was nestled on campus no more than 50 yards from my dorm room. It was a brick, Renaissance-style chapel that was built in the early 1930s. The vaulted barrel ceiling, the stained glass windows displaying images of women from the Bible, and the slate floor made us feel like we were thrown into Southern Europe each time we attended the private services. The split area around the alter opened up to the choir as well as the high altar; it was an intimate yet extraordinary space. And, because we were required to attend chapel six times a week, it gave me plenty of opportunities to borrow a candle or two as I worked my acolyte duties.

By this time, I had my own room on the corner of Dabney Hall, and Karen was stationed directly above me in her single room. We devised a pulley system that consisted of nothing more than a bucket and a rope so that we could stay in constant touch with each other during study hall or beyond "lights out." But it was study hall that really gave me the time to be creative with my candles.

With a single strike of a match, I lit the long acolyte candle and watched the flicker with a mesmerizing gaze. The slow melting of the wax was much more fascinating and satisfying to me than studying Latin. I turned the candle parallel to the old wooden floor and stared into the flame as the hot liquid began to slowly drip onto the ground creating a round pool of hot wax. This made a perfect bed to nestle the bottom of my taper candle. Like magic, the wax set cold and braced the candle in an upright position like I was originally holding it. I found a wood-cased, No.2 HB graphite pencil and the small pack of marshmallows I had purchased from a "Deli run." I used the pencil as a roasting stick and stacked a couple of marshmallows on the end of my pencil. I sat cross-legged, facing my flame and began to prepare what would become one of the most satisfying treats I had ever tasted. I blew out the candle and began to study Latin.

I could tell that the knock on my door was not that of a dorm mom because it carried a confident determination with it. It only lasted a moment and then, within seconds, I was face to face with Ms. Gibson. Now, Ms. Gibson was not someone you ever wanted knocking on your door. She was a combination of Ms. Wagoner and my father, and she was, quite rightly appointed, Dean of Students. She stood there at my doorway, arms crossed, and began to softly but authoritatively speak to me. The sweat started to bead up inside my t-shirt, and without control, and through a trembling voice, I confessed my misadventure to her.

Ms. Gibson spoke in a way that fixated my eyes onto her lips as they moved in slow motion. She did not lecture me. Instead, she sat down beside me, cross-legged. With slight tears in her eyes, she told me a story about a forest fire that erupted years earlier, just a few miles away from our school. She talked to me about my fascination with fire and about how some people were so fixated that they could become obsessed and even turn into pyromaniacs. She defined the word for me by using detailed stories of personal experiences from her own life. She pulled at my heartstrings, and that was it. I was humiliated, remorseful, humbled and filled with regret. I loved her so much for not yelling at me or for not calling further attention to the matter. I forever hold her in the highest regard and vowed never to disappoint her again.

Nancy Hilliard* Joyce
August 10, 2004 | Atlanta, GA

❝ You touched my life in ways you will never know. You will always be with me in my memories of days at Chatham Hall.

With Love,
Nancy Hilliard* Joyce
Class of 1991

Ms. Gibson died in 2004 at the young age of 69. On her obituary page, there was an image of a candle which read, "*light a candle in Connie Gibson's memory.*" The irony I felt lighting a candle for her that day was filled with both tremendous emotion and deep admiration for someone who acted as a parent when mine could not, and for this, I am forever grateful.

Chapter 15
CAMBRIDGESHIRE

"There are thousands of inspirational stories waiting to be told about young women who yearn for a great education. They are stories of struggle and stories of success, and they will inspire others to take action and work to change lives."

- Soledad O'Brien

By the time I reached my senior year, I had finally begun to adapt to the routines and processes of boarding school life. Academics were going relatively well, I felt both confident and secure in my home away from home, and I had just been voted senior class President. Then, sometime around the middle of October, I got wind of a program called Woodberry Forest in Britain. It was an overseas academic program that chose six male students from an all-boys boarding school in Virginia as well as one girl from six additional neighboring single-sex boarding schools in Virginia. Essentially, twelve students had the opportunity to study abroad for their last semester of school.

I distinctly remember wanting to take this risk and change my life around a bit. The application consisted of grade submissions and extensive writing about why you should be chosen for the adventure abroad. I eagerly applied and was surprisingly accepted as the Chatham representative. In January of my senior year, I packed up my things and flew to St. Neots, England, nestled within the county of Cambridgeshire, to live and study overseas with a local family and eleven other students. Our courses consisted of Shakespeare, British government, and Architecture.

We studied and were taught from the home of Richard and Wendy MacKenzie. Their Woodberry Forest in Britain program took us to places I would have never dreamed existed before I traveled there. Each morning, Mr. Mac would wake us up at the break of dawn with the clank of a loud dinner bell.

He'd usher us outside his modest castle-like Cotswold home for our daily jog down his long and winding backcountry road in St. Neots. As the fog lifted against the English backdrop, we'd slowing embrace the morning while dew drops collected onto our cheeks. Following our daily chores and after breakfast was eaten, we'd have a few minutes to change and get ready for school which was taught in his living room.

Thirteen wooden cane chairs were arranged in a circle, one for each of us plus Mr. Mac. Oftentimes, he would teach us directly from his living room and other times we'd venture out and around the United Kingdom to get real-world experiences. We traveled to Stratford-upon-Avon, in England's West Midlands, to study William Shakespeare. We'd read poetry and recite plays in full accent while dissecting Shakespeare's words under a theoretical microscope.

As a precursor to traveling to Wales and learning about Dylan Thomas, Mr. Mac assigned *Under Milk Wood* for us to read. We sat in a small, dimly lit tavern with a fireplace and theatrically read aloud the entire book to one another so we could feel its full impact. I will never forget traveling to the rolling hills of Bath, in Southwest England, and absorbing the beauty that overcame me at that time. We learned about Roman baths and heard stories of leprosy while visiting 18th-century Georgian hot springs. Both the sights and sounds were indelible and mesmerizing to my senses.

While back in St. Neots, we were introduced to traditional cuisine like Welsh rarebit and potato leek soup. Wendy made fresh scones every morning, and I even drank my first taste of sherry on Valentine's Day while standing inside their living room. When in London or larger cities, Mr. Mac would let us partake in cider drinking with limited consumption. I didn't particularly care for the taste of it, but the mere fact that he allowed us to try alcohol while at boarding school was invitation enough for me to live in the moment.

Living and studying overseas instilled in me the confidence I needed to head to college and start yet another chapter in my life. In fact, dropping myself into the unexpected would become something I began to crave. I became bored quickly with routines and needed to mix up the status quo. The result of this newfound fascination and need for change came in different forms as my life continued to progress.

Returning to Chatham Hall, I was able to finish the year strong. I was accepted into Wofford College, which was in my home state of South Carolina. Upon graduation, I was awarded the Senior Art Award as well as the overall Senior Class Award. As the rector read the description of the girl who would receive the Senior Class Award, my parents looked at each other with widened eyes. It has been told by my father that Mom said, "*I wonder who that could be?*" and Dad replied to her without hesitation, "*It sounds just like he's describing Nancy.*" Either way, the idea of hope for my future was beginning to fill the minds of my parents. This recognition not only gave me the confidence to persevere but it also provided me with the strength I would unknowingly need for the years ahead. I left Chatham with a strong foundation of friendships to last me more than three lifetimes. And for this, if nothing else, I am forever grateful.

Chapter 16
THROUGH THE FOG

"With the pride of the artist, you must blow against the walls of every power that exists, the small trumpet of your defiance."

- Norman Mailer

I leapt into the summer after boarding school graduation as if it were the last one of my life. I persuaded my parents that I should attend summer school in Boulder, Colorado. After all, they would be less than 45 minutes away from me in Denver. My responsible first cousin, Charles, was already enrolled in college there. It seemed to be the perfect place for me to reside for eight weeks. He already had an apartment set up and was kind enough to accept me as his summer roommate. I signed up for possibly the most straightforward course available in the curriculum. I planned to take this credit from The University of Colorado Boulder and transfer it to Wofford College so that it would "free me up a bit" from extra coursework. One class. Psychology 101.

I started strong. I was excited about being in a college classroom environment with both males and females. On the first day, I sat somewhere in the middle of the auditorium-like classroom. I was intimidated by the campus as I wasn't used to class sizes where the teacher didn't know my name. We had signed up with our social security numbers and apparently, that was how he identified us during our tests. I made a point to walk down the carpeted stadium stairs to introduce myself to the professor after class on the first day, so that he'd know my name. That would be the last time we would ever speak.

Following my overzealous first day, I attended the class a handful of times, just to get additional homework assignments or to take the occasional test. But that wasn't really my purpose during the summer of 1991. It was the first time I was able to make decisions independently for myself and by myself. This was the summer of discovery and freedom.

That summer, I watched at least a dozen sun rises from the top of Boulder Canyon. I participated in Native American-like drum circles, I discovered sweat lodges and met some of the most eclectic people on the planet. I traveled to Telluride, befriended homeless people, enjoyed music festivals, slept under the stars and declared myself a vegetarian. For a large majority of that summer, I was completely independent of all authority. I gained some insight into life and became wide-eyed to all that the world had to offer. I lived the life of a hippie and barely passed my Psychology course with a C-, which was just enough to give me the three credits I needed to use at Wofford so I could take one less class in college. I wasn't proud of myself but was relieved that I had squeezed by and not completely wasted everyone's time.

In early August, I flew from Denver, CO to Charleston, SC to spend time with my older sister. Kathryn had recently married Gene Stuart, who was my head swim coach many years back. I was friends with his little brother, so their marriage seemed very comfortable to me. Gene was now enrolled in the Medical University of South Carolina, and their future together had just begun. I was in their new home, sitting at their wooden kitchen table, when I signed up for my first semester classes at Wofford College.

I flipped through the course catalog without a care in the world. It was like shopping for back-to-school clothes. I was naïve, undaunted and overly confident as I worked on my course load. I licked the envelope to seal and mail my class choice information off to the administrative office in Spartanburg. Inside that envelope, my 1st-semester fate was sealed: Statistics (at 8 AM on Monday mornings), Chemistry, Psychology 201, Physics and Art History.

A piece of cake.

Chapter 17

1.02

"Failure is simply the opportunity to begin again.
This time more intelligently."
- Henry Ford

I showed up for college unlike the rest of the students. I was a Southern girl arriving from a single-sex boarding school who believed she was carved out of the Rocky Mountains. I wore my Patagonia shorts and oversized outdoorsy T-shirts with my Birkenstocks every single day. Often, I would wear my cowboy hat and hiking boots regardless of the fact that we were barely in the foothills of South Carolina. I quickly sought out other people who looked like they also colored outside the lines of life. And, there I was, away at college, partying like a rockstar, seven days a week.

It didn't take me long to realize that staying out late on Sunday night while heading into an 8 AM Statistics class the following morning wasn't the best idea. I think even without feeling like I had the flu, I would have had a difficult time grasping the complexities of the class, but this certainly wasn't helping me or my case as a freshman in college. Mr. Robinson was kind enough to let me also attend his Wednesday afternoon classes. He told me that he would allow me to take tests on both days, giving me the average of my test grades, to help me out a bit. It did not help.

In addition to my Statistics class, the course pressure of Chemistry, Physics, Advanced Psychology, Art History and late nights soon became an overwhelming workload for me. My advisor pulled me aside within the first 12 weeks and suggested that I was perhaps at the wrong college. We talked at length about how maybe I should be at a Visual Arts school rather than a Liberal Arts school. He also said, quite frankly, that I could not stay at Wofford if things didn't dramatically change. When my grades reached my parents at the end of the first semester, emotions began to get incredibly grave back at home. We were in Colorado for Christmas when Mom and Dad sat me down for a little chat.

With my report card in their hands, they laid down the black and white 1.02 typewritten number the school had mailed to them. It was unbelievable. Although I had been completely aware of my grades the entire 1st semester, it made my head spin looking at my unfathomable GPA. I squirmed in my chair and braced myself for a complete lockdown from my parents. I knew that their inevitable anger was more than justified at that point. I felt that I deserved and would understand if they grounded me for life.

Mom and Dad sat for a while in silence. They just looked at me. They seemed to be studying my face as if I were a rare bird they had just discovered on the side of the road. Then, Dad slowly began to speak. His words flowed out like molasses, and I leaned towards him trying to pull the words out of his mouth so I could understand my fate. I soon realized that this talk carried a certain unrecognizable resolve with it. Rather than being authoritative and directive, they seemed exhausted and contemplative. Both of my parents showed extreme pity towards me and were undeniably saddened that I was struggling so much in college. At this particular juncture, *my parents said something to me that would forever change the course of my academic and career-driven life.*

Dad took a deep inhale as he looked at me with an undeniable lump in his throat. He then explained that he had saved up enough money so that I could stay in college for five years if that is what I needed to do to finish my degree. With glassy eyes, he hugged me tight and let me know that no matter what, he would be there for me and would not, for his life, ever give up on me or my education. The deep anguish that swelled up in my mom's face was overwhelming, and waves of shame and embarrassment began to suffocate me. I nearly drowned in tears that night as I fell asleep in my basement bedroom.

They think I am stupid. This was what I kept repeating to myself. *They think I am stupid and are giving me everything they have in their bank account just to ensure that I finish college. They think I'm dumb and feel sorry for me.* It was with this strength of conviction that I finally turned my "freedom pass" around and began to prove to them that I was not a complete waste to society.

With this renewed strength and steadfast determination, everything began to change. I admitted to both myself and my parents that I had wasted an entire semester and the past summer enjoying life a little too much. As important as it must have been to my development as an individual, I had consciously made many mistakes and immature decisions that affected much more than just my grades. In hindsight, I would have been an ideal candidate for a gap year. I needed a year, after leaving boarding school, to explore my freedom, make mistakes, mature and redirect my attention. I hated that I had done this at my parent's expense. The guilt was nothing short of overwhelming.

If Freud were to have analyzed my situation, he would have said that I was over-exercising my Id during my first semester at college and it was time for me to bring my Superego into focus. I did just that and made well above a 3.25 my second semester freshman year and began to fall back in sync with the love of learning. I decided to major in Art History and spent most of my time analyzing architecture and historical paintings. I started creating again and found myself inspired by the photographs of Edward Curtis. I had my first ever solo art exhibit in the Sandor Teszler Library in 1993. The pieces were all on handmade paper, drawn in charcoal and of Native American influence.

Chapter 18
THE CONTINENTAL DIVIDE

"The knowledge that you have emerged wiser and stronger from setbacks means that you are, ever after, secure in your ability to survive."

\- J.K. Rowling

Historically speaking, I think that whenever parents found their children acting uncontrollably, they would turn them towards the instructive ways of nature for guidance. This is precisely what happened to me following my freshman year in college. The National Outdoor Leadership School (N.O.L.S.) was a place where you not only acquired class credit for learning about the stars, animal tracks, and bear droppings but also an organized way in which teenagers could find themselves by first getting lost. The philosophy was simple: learning to live in unison with nature. Easy enough.

The trek lasted thirty days, and the rules were straightforward. You were not allowed to pack deodorant, toilet paper, razors, food, mirrors or make-up. Only the absolute necessities. You were allowed a backpack, a sleeping bag, a pair of sturdy leather hiking boots, a raincoat, 3 T-shirts, 3 pairs of shorts, 3 pairs of underwear, 1 pair of long pants, 1 set of gators, 1 pair of gloves, a water bottle, iodine tablets, a hat, 1 long-sleeved shirt and 1 winter jacket. The goal was that you shouldn't carry more than half of your body weight. But, carry was precisely what you would be doing with all that you packed. And, once you were packed, you were required to unpack in front of the guides so that they could confiscate any extraneous or "contraband" items. At 65 lbs., my pack was as lean as was physically possible. I was ready.

My group left out of Lander, Wyoming and headed into the Wind River Range. We were prepped to hike over 300 miles, crossing the Continental Divide and trekking through terrain which we were told would range from glaciers to lush, green fields of grass and wildflowers. There were very few trails. Seven boys and seven girls, ranging from ages 16-18 years old, two instructors and a handful of topographical maps. We were met midway, after fifteen days, in the middle of a mountain range, with a few mules that would replenish our dehydrated food and pack out our trash.

The struggle was the most visceral and innate pressure I'd ever experienced in my life. I was challenged physically, emotionally and socially. We walked ten to fifteen miles every day for a month straight. The gnats and mosquitos were almost unbearable. At 12,120', we crossed Indian Pass which consisted of traversing glaciers, hiking through snowfields, using ice axes, withstanding below freezing temperatures, enduring blood-filled boots, falling into waist deep snow, getting lost in whiteouts, crossing crevasses and scaling boulders. We learned to build a fire from twigs without a lighter or match, to bake bread without an oven, about fish physiology, how to treat severe hypothermia, to understand a mountain's ecosystem, to treat a person in shock, to become a good leader and to identify animal prints. We were taught astronomy, geology, weather patterns and high altitude first aid.

I remained true to myself and honest in my ways. I gave it my all and was focused on the Earth more than anything else in my path. I learned, I laughed, I secretly cried. I was scared, I was brave, I was freezing, the mosquitoes made me feel insane, I was overwhelmed, and I was exuberant. I watched a boy, who couldn't take the pressure of it all, be escorted off the mountain by a helicopter and I also watched two young kids fall in love with each other. I felt terrible for the boy who couldn't make it because I knew that his parents had sent him to overcome obstacles. I was annoyed as Hell at the two that fell in love. I wanted the trip to be pure, and that was the only thing that got in my way. But I let it go. It was my opportunity to grow independently and honestly, and for this reason, the trip was a genuine success.

Chapter 19
THE GERMAN CONVENT

"I am strong because I've been weak.
I am fearless because I've been afraid.
I am wise because I've been foolish."

- Anonymous

I think the most unexpected thing my parents encouraged me to do was to travel throughout Europe with two of my best childhood friends when I was twenty-one years old. My dad was offered a job he couldn't refuse, so my parents decided to live abroad for several months. It seemed like perfect timing for this opportunity. It was 1993 and the summer before my junior year in college. From the outsider's perspective, I was plenty mature but at the same time, extremely carefree.

Tres and Margaret were my compadres. Mom

and Dad had set the tone. They decided to give me $30 a day for a 10-day trip. Margaret's and Tres' parents followed suit. We each had $300 in our pockets, a little extra for "emergency," a backpack and a random itinerary of which countries we wanted to travel.

Most interestingly, perhaps, was the recent signing by 12 countries in Europe of the Maastricht Treaty. With this establishment of the European Union, girls all over Europe were now showing off their freedom by wearing less conservative clothing and the World Cup was underway. Additionally, on January 1st of 1993, Czechoslovakia was split into both the Czech Republic and Slovakia. Short-shorts were the newest and hottest accessory, and there was an exuberance about the countries we visited that was difficult to pinpoint. Luckily, the three of us were all going through a "hippie" stage, so we didn't attract too much-unwanted attention. Long skirts, Patagonia jackets, T-shirts, straggly hair, no make-up…that was our thing. Europe at that time was similar to what I would imagine the '60s were like

Margaret, Me and Tres map planning.

in America. It was an opportunistic time for us to travel through Europe and fortunately a relatively safe place to let your children explore without too much concern.

We traveled through The Netherlands, Austria, Switzerland, The Czech Republic, Germany and Belgium in just under two weeks. With a Eurail Pass and only $30/a day allocated to each of us, we were compelled to sleep in youth hostels if we wanted to have any money left over to eat or explore. Within those ten days, we visited concentration camps, graveyards, vineyards, lush gardens, beer gardens, joined hiking tours, ate local cuisine, bought T-shirts and traveled by train, boat and bike.

I distinctly remember the paradoxical feeling of happiness while visiting a Swiss cemetery. Beautifully polished headstones sat between the lush, green and immaculately curated grass. Wildflowers freckled the panorama as we watched cows graze in the distance. The clean smell of mountain air flowed through the fields. Each headstone had a portrait or photograph framed securely in the center of the deceased family member. Fresh annual flowers were planted directly in front of them. Colors and light filled the space, and ironically, we felt as if life surrounded us.

On this same path, but contrary to our experience while visiting the cemetery in the Alps of Interlaken, we stayed a couple of nights in Germany. We felt obliged to visit Dachau before heading to Munich that evening. This was the first Nazi concentration camp that was opened in Germany. We quickly learned that over 200,000 prisoners and 30,000 deaths were documented there during its twelve years of use as a concentration camp. The prisoners included Jehovah's witnesses, homosexuals, immigrants, "race polluters" arrested by the criminal court and people born of Jewish descent. The eerie feeling and bleak gray atmosphere were still present when we visited there. All three of us were profoundly grief-stricken and unilaterally experienced an overwhelming desire for empathy as we walked away with a much clearer insight into the world as we once understood it.

That same evening, we found a convent that would let the three of us spend the night for only $7/person. It was much cheaper than the typical hostel dorm room. The rooms were sparse. Painted concrete walls, three single beds with iron headboards, pure white bed linens and a stark mirrorless bathroom positioned at the end of the hallway for all the guests to share. There was only one simple rule: a midnight curfew. We considered that an easy guideline and knew we would without a doubt be back before 12 AM. It had already been an emotionally long day, so we were prepared to have a low-key evening. We signed up for two nights, knowing that it was our best savings option and felt confident the curfew would keep us in check.

We celebrated our savings by visiting the Hofbräuhaus that evening with some soft pretzels, a cheese plate, a shared Wienerschnitzel and a few beers. We made friends with locals, laughed a lot and the clock seemed to stand still for us. In reality, the time had moved on, regardless of how it felt. We gathered our belongings and briskly jogged, half hysterically laughing, back to the convent hoping that they were not completely stringent about being a few minutes past midnight. Finally reaching the traditional and stark-like building, we rattled the doors, tapped on some windows and then desperately found a payphone booth to call the convent operator. No one answered.

The three of us stood silently for a moment realizing we had been locked out of a monastery. It was close to 1 AM, and we were worried there would be no place at all to find sleep that night. Creatively and desperately we combined our emergency cash, made several pleading phone calls and finally, much to our relief, Tres found us a rather fancy hotel a few miles across the city. We narrowly averted sharing a metal park bench that evening in the middle of Munich, while our backpacks slept safely in a convent behind securely locked doors.

Chapter 20
RESURGENCE

"Failure is success if we learn from it."
- Malcolm Forbes

With a resurgence of energy and direction, I returned to Wofford with an unwavering plan. I joined the cross-country team and with resolute focus and pure determination, and I made the Dean's List during the final two years of college. I was back. I was slowly learning to balance my social life with studying while staying healthy and having fun.

The previous year, I had traveled to Italy with a group of Art History students to study Architecture. Spanning and scouring cities like Rome, Florence, and Venice, I began to discover rich undulating lines of design within physical structures. There was a renewed sense of self that I found on the walls of museums and within the historically rich streets of Italy. I felt alive and connected to the artists of the past and fascinated with their lives.

Because mid-term internships were encouraged by Wofford College, in January 1994, I applied for and was accepted, along with my great friend Amy, to study Native American basketry at the Denver Art Museum. We would work directly under Nancy Blomberg, the Chief Curator of Native Arts.

I remember arriving for the 1st day of "work" at the museum and noticing the building had several oddly shaped windows. I likened it to, at that time, Notre Dame du Haut, the small Roman Catholic, post-modern chapel located in Ronchamp, France. But, this building was many times larger than the chapel in France that I had learned about during my architecture class at Wofford. The thrill of discovering what was behind the walls was nearly palpable.

We followed Mrs. Blomburg down a cold aisle towards her basketry section. Several rows of metal beams held crossbars of plywood planks which stored all of the artifacts. We assisted as the curator slowly pulled the plastic covers off of the intricate baskets. Several hundred tribal baskets, all individually painted and each designed for a different purpose. Amy and I were the ones who would get to transfer them. We carried each basket as if it were the most precious object in the entire museum. Feathers, beads, and bells dangled from the edges of intricately woven forms. I could hardly wait to begin.

We were charged with creating space in an encyclopedic order so that each basket could be seen and recognized as a stand-alone piece. Our plan was to spread the collection of baskets out onto adjacent empty racks and to create breathing room between them. Some baskets were stacked two and three on top of each other. We began with the Navajo tribe and ended with the Zuni tribe. My favorite basketry work came from the Tlingit, Mission Indian and Pomo tribes. These baskets were more intricate than most other tribes. The Pomo baskets were decorated with feathers, beads, and berry colored plant fibers.

Small price tags dangled from each handmade creation. The smaller baskets were priced around $1800, and I felt as if I were handling repurposed gold.

The internship taught me more than just facts about artifacts. It was the kind of learning that would stay with me and steer my life in a direction that would lead me on a path to becoming my true self. Upon returning to Wofford, I not only strove to be a better person, but I also found that I had acquired a sincere desire to respect and understand other cultures.

The Native American culture taught me to be and feel more independent. They were comforted by their spirits and had individual spirits for each facet of their lives. They only worried about their problems and not the problems of others. They were peaceful, and they were honest. The land, the air, and the trees were alive to them. They cared dearly for their surroundings, and they loved one another more than themselves.

During my final semester, I sat down with my dad, and he said quite frankly, "I've been scouring the papers in the Help Wanted section, Nancy, and not one of them is looking for an Art History major. What in the Hell do you *really* plan to do with your life?" Shortly after we spoke, I applied to graduate school. I decided that I would get a Master of Arts in Art Education with a license to teach k-12.

I was accepted into the Master's programs for both The University of South Carolina and the University of New Mexico. South Carolina was my safe choice, and New Mexico was my leap of faith, long-shot daredevil choice. My parents were now living in Atlanta, so Albuquerque was an unknown land to me in a different time zone. As soon as I was accepted into UNM, I felt immediate fear and paralysis. I couldn't logically make this decision on my own.

That summer I flew to see Kathryn. She and Gene were now living in Florida. I was hoping for her opinion or guidance on the matter, but she kept asking me questions about how I felt. She finally instructed me to sit down with a sheet of paper and write down the pros and cons of each school so that

I could decide for myself. I pulled a folded napkin from her kitchen drawer and drew an uneven line down the center tearing a small hole in the middle of the thin paper. I knew where this was going and I was afraid of the outcome.

After completing the list, I reluctantly announced that I was heading out West. I knew I'd be selling myself short if I took the comfortable and predictable route. It felt impulsive and exciting for me to make this calculated risk. I was ready to get outside of South Carolina again. I knew I needed to meet people from other parts of the country and climb out of my comfort zone so I could finally grow up. And, in the back of my mind, I was still chasing Georgia O'Keeffe's ghost.

Chapter 21
WATERMELON SUNSETS

"If you can't figure out your purpose,
figure out your passion. For your passion will
lead you right into your purpose."
-Bishop T.D. Jakes

I arrived in New Mexico with a mountain bike and a car full of used clothing that I had joyfully purchased over the years from second-hand stores. Old man's pants, that were a few sizes too large, made me feel unscathed and relaxed. My vintage faux-fur vest made me feel alive. It was all I needed to begin my journey in this unfamiliar place. I had found my one-bedroom apartment on the Internet. Sight unseen, I discovered my way to the parking lot and went directly to the management office for the key. This was a giant step into adulthood. I could hardly wait to begin this new chapter.

I explored my way through Albuquerque the first week before graduate school classes began at UNM. I quickly found the Double Rainbow Café, located in the Nob Hill area near school, and it became my second home. I rode my bike or walked there with a book or a sketch pad so that I could seem interesting to others but secretly scan the room for a human connection of some sort. It was both intimidating and fascinating being in a town where no one knew my name.

Once classes began, I remember friendships falling quickly into place. I was surrounded by a group of like-minded graduate students who had the same drive and passion as myself. I found a part-time job at a local juice shop called 20 Carrots that was owned and run by Christie Brinkley's brother, a nutritionist from California. We served things like brown rice, tabouli, fresh carrot juice, hand-made organic soups and hummus wraps. For me, in the mid-90s and coming from the South, this seemed to be the beginning of the health craze. I know now that the West Coast and Midwest were a bit more advanced than the fast food mentality that the deep South had adopted at that time.

Academics didn't seem overly taxing because I was finally doing something that I genuinely loved. I was taking a handful of intriguing classes that gave me the desire to excel. One particular studio class consisted of throwing porcelain vessels. The professor who taught us had studied under Sensei Manji Inoue of Arita, Japan and provided emphasis on the use of handmade tools and the potter's wheel spinning clockwise. The composition of porcelain was like nothing I had previously felt. Compared to other stoneware or earthenware, the milky white clay had absolutely no tooth whatsoever. It was silky, cold and damp when we'd pull it from the barrels to knead. The process of wedging the clay was an art in and of itself.

In preparation for wheel work, we were required to use our upper body strength to rotate the porcelain clay on the table in a particular rhythmic and repetitious way as to release all of the bubbles. This process could take up to thirty minutes to prepare. Sometimes, it would have to be repeated. I remember watching my tenured classmates knead their porcelain clay with ease. I became restless and frustrated with the preparatory process much of the time, but soon realized it was *this* meditative activity that became almost more valuable than the throwing, pulling and shaping on the wheel. The wedging process was what gave the porcelain the translucent and vitreous quality I eventually began to value in the finished product.

Besides porcelain work, I dove into multiple disciplines such as raku ware firing, sculpting earthenware clay busts, sterling silver jewelry casting from hand-made wax molds, Native American Art History, the Philosophy of Art, etc. In between my graduate school classes and my part-time job, I approached an outdoor store and started rock climbing on weekends with their staff. It was then that I decided that I was always meant to be a rock climber. With the money I'd saved up from my part-time job, I bought a harness, rock climbing shoes, 100-

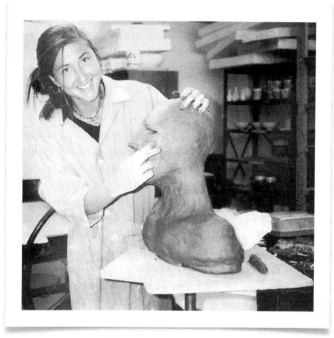

University of New Mexico MA Program, 1996

foot rope and several carabiners. I wanted to look the part for my newfound outdoor sport.

I made an honest effort to wake up early on most Saturday mornings so that I could watch the sun rise over the Sandia Mountain range. I must have rock climbed and mountaineered Sandia Crest Trail a dozen times before I decided that the gear looked much cooler in my closet or hanging on my wall. I had never been a morning person anyway. I kept running for exercise and started doing the Cindy Crawford workout on VHS tape cassette. It was easier to be guided by my own schedule rather than waking up at dawn to meet someone else's, and I soon discovered that the sunsets were even better than the sunrises. The color was otherworldly and beyond the spectrum of anything I had ever seen. The half past 6 o'clock light reflecting against the Sandia granite would turn a gorgeous shade of glowing watermelon. The sky would illuminate, and the feeling of limitless horizons would swell over me.

Mexico wasn't that far away so it was inevitable that I would visit it at some point while I was in graduate school. The timing seemed ideal when an old friend from Asheville, NC flew out to see me. The weekend escape was decided within hours of her arrival. Without solid plans, we decided to drive to El Paso, Texas through Truth or Consequences, New Mexico via the Rio Grande River. Arriving in El Paso, we found an old motel and parked the car in the lot and began to walk south. With backpacks slung onto our shoulders, we set out to find the Mexican border. We traveled over 2 miles on foot, on a highway, alongside cars towards the U.S. Border Patrol at the Mexican border. To this day, I have no idea how or why they let two young American girls walk into Mexico. But, they did. With ease.

We arrived in Juárez by late afternoon and were hell-bent and determined to find sombreros before starting out on our random and delirious journey. As I recall, after several laughing fits later, we successfully found them along with sarongs and other cheap stuff we felt necessary for our trip. Feeling complete with our oversized, colorful, touristy sombreros on top our "cabezas," we ventured out to find margaritas and Mexican food. With broken Spanglish and while channeling the new mid-90s animated show, *Beavis and Butt-head*, we trekked our way through Mexico for 48-hours straight. All I can say is that God was *really* looking after both of us when we arrived safely back to our car, which was still standing alone in the seedy motel parking lot underneath the warm Texan sun.

I grew up a lot while I was in Albuquerque. And by growing up, I mean that I experienced a few hard life lessons. I had arrived in New Mexico mostly unsophisticated and sheltered from both poverty and crime. However, I experienced each of these during my two years there. I'd ride my bike to school most mornings. Parking a car was next to impossible on campus and tickets were handed out liberally if you didn't feed your meter the second it expired. There were bike racks all over campus, and it had seemed to be the most practical and economical way to travel. However, naïve to the fact that Albuquerque was filled with an eclectic melting pot of individuals, I filed out of class one morning to find only my front bike tire waiting for me. It was the first time I had ever been robbed, and I must have stood in the same position for at least 5 minutes. I watched as students came and went, looking at me pitifully like I was a child left at preschool for the first time. No one cared.

I swallowed hard and walked quickly to a pay phone booth to call my mom, but she didn't answer. I eventually found my way to the campus police to file a report. Deep down, I knew they couldn't do anything about my missing bike. I could tell by their response and casual demeanor that it was something that happened all the time. They explained to me, because I begged for information, that it was most likely being sold somewhere in a different neighborhood and that I should find a new means of transportation.

I stiffened my upper lip and chalked it up to a lesson learned. I felt a little worldlier after that and began to watch my back a little. Several weeks passed before I resorted to my old and careless habits. It was early afternoon on Friday and was returning home from the supermarket. I quickly took a handful of groceries from my car. My apartment was only on the second floor and right around the corner from where I parked. It was no more than a 30-yard walk. As I came back for the second load, I realized that my fanny pack, which held my wallet, rolls of film and school ID were all missing from my car. I looked around and saw some teenagers down the block rolling away on skateboards. I had to assume it was them but I wasn't completely certain. It made me feel better to think that it may have been kids rather than a lurking adult, even though I once again felt scared and victimized. This time, I didn't bother going to the police.

Always looking for an opportunity to make a living from my art education, I found an advertisement in the *Albuquerque Journal* asking for someone to recreate a street sign for their hotel. I headed to Kinko's Signs and More and immediately had business cards made for myself. I was now "Hilliard Designs". My logo was a tube of paint. I contacted the hotel, drove out there a day later and made an appointment to meet with the owner of the hotel. I had absolutely no experience in design, commercial real estate or contracting. I got the job.

The original sign was 14 feet long and 8 feet tall and slightly curved at a 30° angle. It stood at the end of the hotel entrance and was made of concrete. My job was to create a design, logo, and signage that would "glow with a shadow effect" from the streets to attract new potential hotel guests. I was allowed to create a new logo but within the confines of the old and without defacing the concrete wall. Without one iota of knowledge about this type of job, I attacked the project like it was the most important thing I'd ever do in my life. I visited manufacturers, contractors, and design teams. I asked hundreds of questions, created a spreadsheet of comparisons and did research on weather resistance, transparency, electrical hookups, pricing, logistics of completion, materials needed, etc. A few months later, I approached the owner of the hotel again with my proposal. I got the green light and my first paycheck advance for the project.

I had met some interesting people during my inquiry process that I knew I would need on my team. My first and only hire was a seventeen-year-old boy who was the son of a contractor I had met a few weeks back. He was knowledgeable, savvy, hard-working and cheap. I paid him $5.00/hour, which was $.25 higher than minimum wage at the time. He was thrilled. Together, we worked countless hours devising a plan to create a sign that would "glow from the road." I ended up going with a thick, waterproof thermoplastic. I had the finished design laser-cut into translucent red plexiglass, and we mounted the sign with steel standoffs. Below the initial design, we positioned mosaic tiles in a pattern

"Souls, Circles & Selves", 1997.

for an added effect. Finally, we installed landscape lighting into the ground below so that it would shoot up under the raised plexiglass, and reflect into the night sky. Task complete. Although it was a successful project, I realized that school needed more attention so decided to leave Hilliard Designs until after graduation.

My graduate school thesis was titled, *"The Assessment of an Affective Art Program Guided*

Toward Increasing a Child's Self-Esteem." It took me several months to write the 15-page paper that focused on ways to increase a child's intrinsic motivation through a non-competitive environment. I emphasized human integrity, character, and accountability. I compared "task-oriented leadership origins" to "ego-focused pawns" with emphasis on The Arts in American schools. I got an A on the final piece, but the professor noted that it was both altruistic and unrealistic. He wished me good luck. Annoyed with his comment, I disregarded him, but something deep within me knew that he may be right.

I completed my student teaching, and with my license to teach k-12, I was now licensed in New Mexico with reciprocity for many other states. I researched jobs in North Carolina, South Carolina, and Georgia. I was ready to be closer to my family for a change, and I wanted to have a plan the second school was out. There was one job, in particular, located in Asheville, North Carolina that caught my eye. The Asheville Art Museum was looking for an

Outreach Curator, so I spent most of my free time vying for the position.

Mom flew out to Albuquerque for my graduation. She met my small group of artist friends, saw where I had lived for the past two years, took some photographs, and I said my goodbyes. We skipped the graduation ceremonies, and with my car packed full of collected second-hand clothing, climbing gear, art supplies, porcelain vases, several blankets and a cow skull, we made our way back across the United States. With my mother mostly behind the wheel, I dreamed of my future as memories of watermelon sunsets faded slowly in the rearview mirror.

Chapter 22
THE RURAL SQUIRREL

*"Let us remember: One book, one pen, one child,
and one teacher can change the world."*
- Malala Yousafzai

I have to assume that a combination of luck, God's grace, and extreme perseverance helped me to land the job at the Asheville Art Museum. It paid one hundred dollars a day and was funded by the City of Asheville from grants received by the museum. I felt like I had hit the jackpot. My job was to travel from Asheville to different rural parts of North Carolina. Every morning, I drove at least 2 hours round trip up and down winding roads into deeply hidden mountain towns. I was assigned a different public school each day of the week, and my charge was to bridge reading, writing and math skills through the reference of our permanent art collection within the museum.

The museum's permanent collection, at this time, mostly consisted of works from Social Realists during the WPA (Works Progress Administration) period. In the mid-1930s, the United States was, of course, in the center of a global economic depression. In an effort to provide financial relief to artists, who were having trouble finding work, President Roosevelt established the WPA. For artists to be considered for the project, they first had to apply for Home Relief in order to prove they were destitute, and then submit samples of their work demonstrating they were actively creating art. Once approved, an artist was paid twenty-four dollars a week.

With 8mm slides of the Asheville Art Museum's permanent collection and a projector in hand, I approached the rural classrooms with daunting yet hopeful ideals. These children, living in the deep hills of North Carolina, were mostly coming from poverty-stricken homes. Their guardians didn't always have enough money to feed them each day.

The students often spoke to me about hunting and eating squirrel as if it were a delicacy. Furthermore, it was apparent and well-known that if disobedience happened in the classroom, it was perfectly acceptable for the principle to paddle the students. Some places in Appalachia made me wonder whether or not The Great Depression had actually ended.

The children were wide-eyed and always excited to see me when I arrived in their classroom. I used paintings from this period to explain concepts and terms such as perspective, portrait, landscape, horizontal, vertical, depth, thoughts of people in the paintings, etc. We wrote stories about the men and women who were portrayed in the portraits. We'd guess their names and imagine their lives outside of the painting, creatively writing about people we would never meet. We discussed perspective, spoke of measurements and did projects that had them using rulers while thinking spatially. Best of all, we collected our opinions and brought them to the table for dissection.

I connected with the children in these rural

schools and enjoyed my commute to and from my one-bedroom home in Chicken Hill, which lay alongside a very steep and winding cul-de-sac in a seedy area of Asheville. I lived on the fringe of the River Arts District, which was really before the Arts District was anything more than artists inhabiting old, broken down warehouses to create their trade with little or no rent. I'd come home from my inspired days of teaching amongst the rural squirrels and would collapse onto my bed. My black Labrador puppy, Chili, would be waiting for me. She was restless and bored. It took everything out of me to get up early, take care of Chili, drive for an hour, teach new kids each day in different schools, drive back home, walk Chili and make supper for myself. I barely had time to create art and would often try to steal hours late into the night so that I could paint or work in my sketchbooks.

It became clear to me that I could not continue to teach for the rest of my life. My voice would become hoarse most afternoons, and my exhaustion was total. As much as I loved people, I discovered at the age of twenty-two that I needed time alone. I needed time outside of the car, out in nature, running trails or just sitting alone with my paintings in order to regroup.

Chapter 23
PEACE CORPS BOY

*"There is nothing in a caterpillar that tells you
it's going to be a butterfly."*
- R. Buckminster Fuller

I completed my tenure at the Asheville Art Museum and immediately began to tutor children at the Huntington Learning Center. I also worked as a hostess at a local restaurant to make sure I was bringing in enough money to make rent and pay my bills. The Huntington Learning Center was great but ended quickly. Within the first week, I was assigned to tutor a young girl named Laura. She had long, wavy strawberry blond hair and porcelain skin with a sprinkle of freckles adorning her cheeks. She was around seven years old. We'd work together on reading and then we'd take a break in the parking lot and play games together. Each time she came to the center, her parents would request me and sooner than later, she became sort of like a baby sister to me. I'd bring bubbles and sidewalk chalk to play with during our breaks.

With a stroke of good fortune, her father decided to hire me directly. This new system consisted of me tutoring Laura each day at her house. I enjoyed working directly with their family which instilled a deep bond between us. Eventually, I began tutoring Laura in her father's law office so that he could continue to work at his practice while his daughter was learning and being entertained. This went on for a few months before he suggested that I work directly for his law office, doing creative marketing to help grow his practice. He had recently joined a group called, The American Academy of Estate Planning Attorneys. He hired me to create new client data and to prepare marketing materials to educate retirees about the importance of proper estate planning. This only lasted about a month before I decided to move to Arizona.

Walter was the reason. I first met him in the Atlanta airport in 1994 on New Year's Eve. I saw him waiting for the same flight that I was about to board to Asheville, NC. He had wavy, shoulder-length, sandy blonde hair and I felt an immediate attraction and connection to him. I started talking to him as we were waiting in line to give our tickets to the flight attendant. It was a small commuter plane, and we were two of about thirteen passengers. We chatted as we boarded and because the flight wasn't full, we sat beside each other. Walter had me laughing almost the entire trip.

I learned during the one hour and fifteen-minute flight that he was a volunteer with the Peace Corps in the Solomon Islands. He would be returning to Guadalcanal in a few days but gave me his address so that we could write to each other. There was something different and fascinating about Walter, and I didn't want to lose touch with him even though I knew it was a long shot that we would ever see each other again.

We ended up writing letters back and forth for

three years. Walter would send me hand-written, detailed stories of his time in the Peace Corps along with fantastic and colorful photographs of his students and island locals. I learned of his setbacks with malaria, and he would describe his living situation and experiences with his students. During the three years that followed, we saw each other once in the late spring of 1995 and then again in December 1997. It was that Christmas, in Colorado, when we decided that we couldn't be apart from each other any longer and it was the summer of 1998 when he was accepted into business school at Thunderbird located in Glendale, Arizona.

Chapter 24
MILK AND HONEY

*"If one dream should fall and break into a
thousand pieces, never be afraid to pick one of those
pieces up and begin again."*
- Flavia Weedn

From 1998 until late 2003, I worked as the Marketing Director of various law firms based out of Arizona, New York, and Atlanta. I would often fly to Los Angeles and work from West Coast offices as well as the occasional jaunt to London offices. I quickly rose up the ranks of more extensive and diversified law firms and earned well into six figures. I was dedicated, committed, creative and determined to please both the attorneys and my national marketing team. And, mostly my father. He was extremely proud of my success. He would send articles to me on a weekly basis and would frequently boast to his colleagues and friends about my work. I felt accomplished!

Walter and I married in January of 2000, and soon afterward we moved to Manhattan driving a small U-Haul with our black lab, Chili. Walter told me he wanted us to be "thrown into the fire" and convinced me that if we could have a successful marriage in New York, we could be successful anywhere. We found an apartment on the 38th floor of The Madison Belvedere, a new high-rise positioned on the corner of Madison Avenue and 29th, located in an up-and-coming area called Murray Hill. Walter found a job on Wall Street, and I worked as the Marketing Director for a law firm in the Rolex building located near Central Park. We lived a simple life, with very little friction and spent the majority of our time just enjoying The Big Apple.

As newlyweds and still without children, Walter and I decided we had time to train for the New York Marathon. We were running six days a week and reserving our extremely long runs for Saturdays. Every single Saturday following our long runs, we would shower and head to Les Halles, our favorite French restaurant for red wine, petite filets, and frites. New York was fantastic for our new marriage, our careers, our health and our emotional well being. We found nooks and crannies within the city and frequently visited speakeasy-esque joints such as Milk & Honey, which was owned by celeb cocktail artist Sasha Petraske. We felt cultured and included in the Manhattan mix.

By late summer, we were up to at least sixteen miles on Saturdays. It was also around this time that my paternal grandmother, Anna, was diagnosed with Stage IV Colon Cancer. In late August 2001, I jumped on a plane to Anderson, SC to spend the weekend with Anna. I recall Anna greeting me by walking slowly into her kitchen to offer me fresh farm picked peaches. I remember leaving for long periods of time to go on runs. Not wanting to end my training, I continued to run long mileage throughout the weekend. I didn't really understand the depths of her pain and suffering. I felt removed from her situation to the point that I now have deep regret. In retrospect, I could see that she was trying to be my hostess and my caring grandmother. I wish I had stayed longer and cared for her, read books to her, played music for her, painted her toenails, found extra help for her or worked to expedite her Hospice care.

I returned to Manhattan from South Carolina, and just two weeks later, the September 11th attacks happened. When we received the news of the first plane hitting one of the twin towers, we all assumed it was a small, single-engine plane that had made poor judgment. But, as the story broke and flowed into our offices, we began to awaken to the reality of it all. I circled my office not knowing whether to run downtown towards our apartment and the towers or stay put near Central Park. Then, I noticed that there was a message blinking on my phone. It was from Walter. He said, "Hey Nancy...I am staring at what I think was a commuter plane accidentally hitting one of the twin towers. We haven't evacuated yet, but I will call you back if we are asked to leave."

I called him back. No answer. Two unsettling hours passed, and by this time, both towers had been hit, and the Pentagon attack had also been reported.

Everything changed.

I immediately left work and began running down 5th Avenue towards our apartment complex in my business suit and heals. I was not alone. Droves of pedestrians were huddled together listening to radios in the middle of New York streets. No taxis or cars could be seen driving in any direction. Cell service was impossible. Every few blocks, I would stop and lean into a group of people for updates. I was panicked. I imagined Walter running into the burning towers and trying to rescue people. Around 42nd Avenue, I began to see men and women emerge with ashes and dust all over their bodies. The experience was surreal and impossible to comprehend. I kept running toward the towers.

There, standing on the corner of 38th and 5th, I saw Walter, salted from the dust of the fallen towers, positioned like a frozen soldier, holding onto Chili's leash. My breath became softer, and I began to cry. He was alive. Between the circumstances of 9/11, my grandmother's fatal diagnosis and our marathon training, I decided I could either break *from* the chaos or *through* the chaos. But, as I had never been one to quit when in distress, I pressed even harder to complete my goal of running the New York Marathon.

Twenty-five thousand runners stood at the starting line, and nearly all of us were wearing "United We Run" buttons or tags somewhere affixed to our clothes. The experience of running 26.2 miles through every borough in New York City, watching firefighters, police officers, citizens and business owners cheer for us was nothing less than life-changing. I am not sure I could have finished strong without the crowd support. I felt unbelievably weightless until about mile eighteen and then my lower back, and right knee started to give out. I had lost Walter at the start of the race. He was out ahead of me somewhere, and it was up to me to get through the last bit alone. I stopped by a medical tent to get sports cream to reduce the swelling in my knee and then carried on knowing that 8 miles were nothing compared to what was already behind me. My body was not as light, but I pushed onward. Around mile twenty-three, I gained a second wind and once again felt weightless. The end was in site with only three miles remaining.

Then a miracle happened on the Upper Eastside of 96th Street by Central Park. I saw Walter. Within the sea of 25,000 people, I saw my husband. He had sprinted ahead of me at the start, and I had found him at mile twenty-three. And, as if he needed a second wind to help him through the marathon, we joined hands and ran the remaining three miles together like it was meant to be…side-by-side. Both exhausted, both sore, both mentally spent. Across the finish line we strode, space blankets wrapped around our shoulders, dizzily drained. We had done it.

Chapter 25
SOUTHERN LIVING

"Define success on your own terms,
achieve it by your own rules, and build a
life you're proud to live."
- Anne Sweeney

For the months that followed 9/11 and the heart-breaking passing of my grandmother, Anna, I began to feel like The City was closing in on me. I didn't sleep well at night. I had mild anxiety about living on the 38th floor, away from my parents, exposed to airplanes and with the life-wind somewhat knocked out of me. We were instructed to evacuate our apartment building several times a week in the middle of the night because of anthrax scares. More frequently than ever, my subway line would abruptly close on the way to work for the same reasons. I needed to get out. I was no longer happy living in Manhattan.

Eventually, I convinced Walter that I needed to move south. My parents were living in Atlanta at the time, and I longed for the comfort of family again. I wanted to feel safe. I quickly transferred to an Atlanta law firm and happily worked as their Marketing Director. But, the transition was not easy. Walter had to stay in New York to help facilitate the sale of his business while I was determined to set up a home for us in Georgia. I felt grown up and satisfied that we'd found a house and a yard. I was excited to be moving into a stage of our lives that felt more like "adulthood." Walter flew home every weekend and I was hopelessly optimistic that he would be able live full-time with me in Atlanta very soon.

After more than a year of living in solitude during the weekdays, we decided that it was time to start our own family. I found myself painting adult elephants, giraffes, and zebras with their calves and foul. I was thirty-three years old and was ready to become a mother. In December of 2003, I gave birth to our first child — a baby girl. The moment I saw her, I decided to retire from the world of law firms and dive into the life of motherhood. My paycheck went to zero, but the emotional rewards were priceless. Claudia was my everything.

"This is boring. Let's have children."

Once her nap time was established, I began to paint again on a regular basis. Walter commuted on the weekends for five years until Claudia turned three years old. And, although they eventually did sell the company, it was under the condition that

Walter would stay with the firm for at least one more year. Soon after the additional year was complete, Walter was offered a job at another financial firm in Manhattan.

I met great friends in Atlanta, spent a lot of time exercising with my mom and renovating my "dream" kitchen. Walter's promotion and move to another trading firm in New York was nothing less than what I felt was an unfortunate turn of events. Nevertheless, we were thankful that he was progressing in his career and knew we needed to have our family together. We sold our house, and I reluctantly moved back north. This time, however, landing in New Jersey.

One year after the move, I gave birth to our son. James was the first boy out of all the children and grandchildren from my parents' side, so it was fun to experience this newfound joy. For the two years that followed, I was nurturing a newborn and a four-year-old, so again, my painting career took a backseat. This was fine with me though because I was the happiest I'd ever been with two healthy children and the four of us all under one roof.

For Christmas in 2008, Walter gave me my first artist website. It was an old-school looking website that felt incredibly practical at that time. It gave me the chance to see all of my work up to that point in one centralized location. At this same juncture, Claudia and James were six and two. And, although I had very little time to paint, we had a designated room in our house for my art studio. Regardless of my inactivity, my studio always seemed to be prioritized over having a guest bedroom, which was never convenient for visitors. But it was my space. A necessity. I often worked spontaneously but was mostly driven by commissions. I was beginning to find my unique style of painting, but the hours I committed to my passion were inconsistent at best.

One late Tuesday evening, Walter looked sideways at me in our bed and asked if I was ready to move back down south. I never *wanted* to move north. So, at first, I couldn't tell if he was kidding. My heart had never left the southeast — I knew I belonged back there. We discussed possibilities for our move. We spoke of Atlanta, Austin, Charlotte, Charleston, Birmingham, Charlottesville, Savannah, and Asheville. Over the next few weeks, we discussed the pros and cons of these cities. We narrowed it down. We made our decision. We were both Southerners at heart and felt determined to raise our kids near their grandparents. And with this unshakable conviction, Walter resigned from working on Wall Street the following day.

We found a house in the mountains that sat on over two acres of land. More than an acre was on a 100-year flood zone but in the summertime, the back meadow would overflow with wildflowers. Walter and my mom planted hundreds of milkweed, and we watched more than twenty monarch butterflies build their cocoons and emerge from their chrysalises before taking off to Mexico. We built a treehouse for the kids, lived on a creek and plowed trails through the field for laser gun wars. We had a zipline that led from the back of the treehouse to the middle of the field. We raised chickens for five years until their unhappy ending thanks to a sly, red fox. Our organic garden provided us with asparagus, mint, peas, tomatoes, squash, and kale. I felt as if we were living inside the pages of a story-book.

The kids were of school age, so I began working as a full-time artist out of a studio in the River Arts District (RAD) based out of Asheville, North Carolina. I dove headfirst into my dream job and wasted no time creating and selling work to both locals and tourists. I began painting subjects that included variations of the wheel. The wheel for me represented the cycle of life. I painted several pieces that included the bicycle wheel, cogs, dandelion clocks, the Ferris wheel, the merry-go-round, the wagon wheel, the water wheel and wind farms.

In February of 2012, just four months after beginning my full-time art career, I received a call from a free-lance writer proposing an article for *Southern Living Magazine.* I was waiting at the window of a Starbucks drive-thru, with both kids sitting in the back seat when an unidentified number rang onto my cell phone. By then, I was used to answering random calls from people who had recently come through my studio looking to purchase paintings. But, this was not one of those calls. The writer had received my business card from another free-lance writer and scouter who evidently had met me and seen my paintings inside my studio. They were interested in my work and my opinion of the Asheville art scene. She was proposing to write an article titled, *Insider's Guide: Asheville's River Arts District.*

I quickly ramped up my website, scoured the Arts District, learned about every single artist living and working in the area, intensified my work schedule and waited for the interview. Since technically speaking, it was my first real press opportunity, I prepared as if I were being interviewed for *Rolling Stone Magazine.* I imagined them researching my life history and asking me about my childhood, detecting every gesture and detailing how I ended up becoming an artist. I toyed with whether or not I would reveal specific compromising stories of my teenage years wondering if that would help to attract additional readers.

The interview day finally arrived. It was sprinkled with a fascinating patchwork of questions, which she thoughtfully stitched together throughout the day. We spent the afternoon talking to each other, walking the streets of the RAD and making conversation with other artists. I did give her quite an earful with my stories of teenage-hood that, thankfully, she chose not to use in the article. However, she somehow captured my personality and most of all, I was officially on the "artist map" when the piece finally landed on shelves in June of that same year. Eventually, this exposure helped me to gain the self-confidence and conviction to keep digging deeper and further into my arsenal of paintbrushes. I started to realize that it was possible to use my art as a way to help others. A platform, of sorts, to expand awareness of those in need.

Chapter 26
PAPER TIGERS

*"The most difficult thing is the decision to act,
the rest is merely tenacity. The fears are paper tigers.
You can do anything you decide to do.
You can act to change and control your life;
and the procedure, the process is its own reward."*
- Amelia Earhart

I assumed that since I landed inside one of the most well-known lifestyle magazines in North America that I'd naturally find confidence and comfort in my work. I thought this opportunity would not only elevate my art but would also allow me to make a more meaningful impact philanthropically. I expected art collectors to seek me out from all over the southeast. I hoped that other artists would contact me for collaborative opportunities and I anticipated an influx in sales.

It was quite the contrary. The elusive nature of the words inside those pages (that most people never even took time to read) led me nowhere but deep inside my own head. In the years that followed, no matter how many journals, newspapers, magazines or front covers my artwork appeared, I continued to feel less than fulfilled and unworthy of public attention.

I would continuously work late into the night, downstairs in my private studio, preparing for the next day which would then solely belong to the public. The sketches, notes and hours upon hours that I would log, in preparation for the next tomorrow, would inevitably find me surrounded by critics. The critics, however, were mostly in between my own two ears. In reality, I felt an overwhelming outpouring of encouragement from the general public. I was back to making nearly the same amount that I made as a Marketing Director at the law firms, but I found myself burning the candle at both ends. I was trying my best to go beyond my limits, which included lack of sleep, over-thinking and being mostly preoccupied with furthering my art career. After all, I had a husband and two children that also needed and wanted my attention.

With some extreme soul searching, sincere prayer and significant introspection, I soon realized that all of these fears and over-dramatizations swimming around inside my head were nothing more than paper tigers. It turned out that the simple act of painting and producing works wasn't completely fulfilling to me anymore. I longed for something more meaningful. I found that I was meeting the needs of *others* by completing works that *they* wanted to purchase but that my own needs were no longer being met.

My newfound desire to paint was satisfied when I relented to the higher calling of me to giving back to those with more significant needs than I had myself. Partnering with charitable causes, in connection with my art openings, became my goal. I wanted collectors to feel that they were receiving more than just a piece of art. I aimed to collaborate with them so we could help society at the same time.

To this end, I consciously switched my mindset and began proactively planning my shows around meaningful themes, rather than just commercial appeal. The world suddenly seemed to spin a bit slower, and not surprisingly, my art took off to an entirely new level. A level where giving back to the community and making a difference became the forefront of my motivation and inspiration. My primary focus became painting in such a way that could inspire children, nurture the environment, and foster the arts.

Chapter 27
THIRTEEN

"We won't be distracted by comparison if we are capti-vated with purpose."
- Bob Goff

With this new perspective on painting, I confidently directed my next series in such a way that giving back became my primary objective. I dedicated nearly all of 2013 to painting thirteen historical and influential women. I gave a portion of my sales to Girls on the Run, a non-profit organization that inspires girls to be joyful, healthy and confident using a fun, experience-based curriculum which creatively integrates running. My purpose with this series was to expose young teenage girls to role models they did not see in the news on a daily basis. Social media was beginning to take over, and I felt that we were all losing direction.

Initially, I made a list of women who had inspired me in my life. My mother was at the top. However, I knew I needed appeal to all young girls, so I decided to pare the list down to just thirteen historical women. This number is symbolic to me on many levels. My birthday lands on 1.31 which is thirteen both backward and forwards. I ran my first half-marathon with my dad on Thanksgiving, and this was, of course, 13.1 miles. Additionally, when a young person turns thirteen, we are immediately considered a teenager. In just one day, twelve turns into thirteen, and we are seen as young adults rather than children. We go from a child with innocent hopes and dreams to an impressionable young adult with ideas and aspirations. A new chapter in our lives. Thirteen.

I wanted thirteen women of variety. I hoped to inspire all young girls who came to my art opening. I wanted to pique the interest of a vast group. I wanted to paint women who had made their lives impressionable starting at a young age. I tried to portray them all at the age of thirteen, whether or not they gained their fame later in life. I wanted these women to feel current and to have a modern-day appeal.

On January 31st, 2014, I not only celebrated my 42nd birthday but I did it with an art opening called THIRTEEN. That evening, I showcased thirteen, larger than life, paintings that were positioned around the room in birth order. I included two mythological women into the mix. I began with Artemis, then Joan of Arc, Queen of Hearts, Queen Elizabeth, Sacagawea, Annie Oakley, Helen Keller, Georgia O'Keeffe, Amelia Earhart, Mother Teresa, Rosa Parks, Eartha Kitt and finally Jane Goodall.

I set up the wooden easels so they'd line the perimeter of the room in semi-circle format. The center of the room was left open for food, wine, and viewing. A young girl by the name of Sarah Tucker sat in the corner of the ballroom strumming her guitar and playing melodic acoustic music. Two tables sat long ways at the opposite end of the semi-circle of easels. On each of the long tables, I had several framed prints for sale. Over two hundred and fifty people arrived at the one-night show which was held at the OMNI Grove Park Inn. Friends from all over, students, teachers, parents, and collectors all came to the opening. Twelve of the thirteen original works of art were sold that evening, and I raised over two thousand dollars for Girls on the Run of Western North Carolina. The tone was set, and I was filled with hope and intention upon giving a portion of my proceeds to help these young girls. From that moment forward, this was my sole purpose.

Chapter 28
TWO WHEELS
AND AN UMBRELLA

*"It takes courage to grow up
and become who you really are."*
- e. e. Cummings

It was October 2014 and close to 2 AM when I was struck with an epiphany while searching on Pinterest for inspiration. I was specifically looking for women with bicycles so I could transform them into paintings when I came across a young girl from Cambodia holding a drawing of a bicycle she'd created in crayon and pencil. Underneath the photo of this young girl, there was a quote from Susan B. Anthony which read, *"Let me tell you what I think of bicycling. I think it has done more to emancipate women than anything else in the world. It gives* women a feeling of freedom and self-reliance. I stand and rejoice every time I see a woman ride by on a wheel...the picture of free, untrammeled womanhood."

I read this quote repeatedly that evening. I was trying my best to carefully wrap my head around and empathize with these women who once felt untrammeled freedom from something as simple as two wheels. Images of ladies with long skirts on bikes began to flood my thoughts.

At the same moment, I realized I had unintentionally been channeling the late 1800s through my paintings over the last few years. I had always been fascinated with women on bikes and had historically portrayed them wearing long skirts or long dresses. It was as if I had been painting these images without knowledge or understanding of *why* I was drawn to them. It was the sense of freedom that I saw in them. The idea that they could feel independent and free from constraints, regardless of their place in the world.

I continued searching. I discovered that the

little girl who had drawn the bicycle with pencil and crayon had just received a bike of her own. She lived in a remote village outside of Siem Reap, Cambodia and that bicycle symbolized both the hope of an education and the promise of safety. I learned that most young girls in Cambodia were not always fortunate enough to receive an education. I discovered that they were generally sent to work in fields alongside their mothers. Often, families could not even afford rice, so daughters were obligated to help their families with labor and forced to quit school. In the unlikely event these girls had parents who were willing and able to sacrifice extra hands tending their fields, the opportunity arose for them to be educated. Still, a young girl traveling alone on foot included multiple risks in a developing country.

As a mother of a young teenage girl, and given my own struggles at that age, I felt compelled to support this cause. I continued my research online and learned that an organization called Lotus Pedals was working to provide bikes to these brave girls. So, around three in the morning, I sent an email to the head of the organization announcing that I was going to have a show called "Bicyclette" which would open in October of 2015. I told them that I wanted to give a percent of all proceeds from the sale of my work to their organization. I would be painting girls with bicycles and women with umbrellas. The girls with bikes would represent untrammeled freedom and the women with umbrellas would symbolize protection from the outside world. With this self-imposed deadline, I gave myself a year to produce the work.

Less than a week later, I received a reply from Lotus Pedals. We set up a meeting so that I could explain my concept to them. They were thrilled to partner with me which gave me additional conviction and momentum. My research began immediately. I scoured articles and websites for information on Cambodian girls. I scoured websites and outlets that provided me with images and visuals of life outside Siem Reap. I took my medium, my process, and my pallet into consideration. I wanted it all to be distinctly removed yet connected to my previous work.

I decided to produce at least 25 paintings over

the course of the year for Bicyclette. Each piece was on a cradled panel rather than canvas. I used a new technique of adhering hand-made paper from Nepal onto the wooden panels. I tore the handmade paper into individual, 4-sided, small and medium shapes. I left the edges of the paper rough and exposed. I then coated the patchwork layers of paper with clear gesso. The handmade paper, the rough edges, the patchwork; they each had a purpose. I considered the turbulent lives of these girls as being the uneven edges of the torn paper. I thought endlessly about their quandary as I painted each piece for the show. I contemplated the girl's tired and chapped hands working in the fields. The undercurrent of each work pulled me in so deeply that my year nearly turned upside down with emotion.

The paintings were all monochromatic. The handmade paper was an Earth tone cream. I sketched in charcoal and chose only one color outside the spectrum of black, white and brown for each work. I had images of Schindler's List swirling throughout my mind where the girl in the red dress appears in only one lightning-fast scene of the black and white movie. I wanted the paintings to be raw. I let my emotions fall in and out of the work so that I could truly empathize with their plight. I felt for the girls in some pieces, and I aligned my thoughts with the mothers in other works. I unintentionally took it beyond my limit. By the time October rolled around, I was spent. I had given absolutely everything to these paintings.

Chapter 29
GO FORTH AND HAVE NO FEAR

"Always be yourself, express yourself, have faith in yourself. Do not go out and look for a successful personality and duplicate it."

\- Bruce Lee

As planned, in October 2015, I had an opening called, *Bicyclette*. Newspapers, prominent magazine articles, social media outlets, alternative periodicals, and fliers had circulated throughout Asheville for several months leading up to the event. At this opening, hosted at the Asheville Art Museum, there were so many people moved by this story that I enabled them to give directly to Lotus Pedals. Additionally, the success of my art sales gave me the opportunity to provide over 100 all-terrain bicycles to young girls in the remote areas of Cambodia.

Less than a month later, my real hero and inspiration, my mother, traveled with me halfway across the world to Cambodia to be part of a bike ceremony outside of Siem Reap. The two of us were both anxious and curious to embark on such a meaningful but distant area in Southeast Asia. The eight separate vaccinations alone were enough to make us turn back. However, determined to help me fulfill my dream, the two of us set off as mothers, daughters, sisters, and wives with hopes of inspiring these girls on the opposite end of the world.

We had heard frightening stories and were initially fearful of traveling to Cambodia. After all, we did not speak the language and were exploring on our own. From mosquitoes to landmines, our Americanized imagery of this distant land had us nervously laughing as we left the Carolinas. I was separating from my children and husband for two weeks and didn't know if I would return home. My daughter, with anaphylactic allergies, would be a day away from us the entire trip, leaving me with paralysis as her caregiver. I felt like we were taking a considerable risk. As a result, I had to convince myself that if something happened to me, at least I left the world trying to help others.

"Go Forth and Have No Fear"

Cambodia captivated all of my senses. The palette range I used within my paintings blended perfectly with the landscape of Southeast Asia. Earth tones swept across the roads which were mostly covered in clay and dust. Monks in bright orange robes walked along the temple grounds. Lush, green rice paddy fields were freckled with floating lotus flowers. Temples and monuments throughout the country seemed like drip castles in the sand from thousands of years past. Women and children, biking in every direction, carried loads of blankets, flowers, and food to sell in the markets. Vast horizons with luminous sunsets, similar to those in New Mexico, filled the skylines. Mischievous monkeys gathered alongside the road like squirrels in rural North Carolina. Tuk-tuks crowded the streets like taxis in New York, and the people were more kind and giving than anyone else I had ever met in the world.

On the day of the bicycle ceremony, my mother and I were picked up from our hotel and escorted in a van, with five others, to a remote Province in Cambodia. Our day-long journey of bumpy and winding roads would take us to Pong Ro Lower Secondary School in the Pong Ro Krom Commune, Jikreng District, Siem Reap Province. Along the route, we passed several rows of small, wooden houses on high stilts above the ground. These house-like huts were without electricity, water or even furniture. Old, dusty floor mats were rolled up and placed against walls alongside minimal interior spaces. Children ran barefoot as they played with stones and tattered ropes. Women could be seen sitting underneath thatched roofs beside small fire pits roasting eggs and boiling rice noodles in lemongrass broth. Working men and women rode on rudimentary bull-pulled carts with old wooden wheels. I felt as if we'd stepped back in time to an unimaginable place. All of a sudden, I could genuinely feel that I was on the other side of the world and close to nothing familiar at all.

Chapter 30
SMART, BRAVE
AND DETERMINED

"Life is a splendid torch which I have for the moment and I want to make it burn as brightly as possible before handing it on to future generations."
- George Bernard Shaw

The van slowly turned down a side road as dry dirt and pebbles spattered up against the sides of our windows. We approached the schoolhouse, and I craned my neck around to see the entrance as we neared the end of the bumpy, grey road. A small, single-story cinderblock building with white chipped paint sat beside what appeared to be a farm shed. The entrance to the schoolhouse was without a sign or any type of markings. The "door" was un-framed but without an actual door. A single painless window sat up to the left side of the entry opening, and small girls peered out of it.

The area in front of the school building was decorated for the bike ceremony. Turquoise and white flowing drapery swept along the pop up yellow tents. Streamers brightened the many rows of folding chairs that were set up facing a line of card tables. The card tables were covered with white tablecloths, and my name sat directly in the center of the front table. To the left of my nameplate was the District Governor and to the right was the Head of the District Department of Education. Behind the table, there were white cardboard signs announcing the ceremony as well as the timed agenda. A microphone was set up on the main table behind my name tag. Within a few short minutes of surveying the area, I realized that I was their guest speaker.

I remembered Susan B. Anthony and reminded myself of what she fought for over 100 years ago. I walked into the schoolhouse and took a short look around the cinderblock room. Less than 600 square feet of space and some chairs occupied the interior four walls. It was completely bare with no supplies, no pencils, no paper, and no decorations throughout the entire room. A few girls were sitting in chairs waiting for the ceremony to begin and looked at me as if they didn't entirely understand who I was or where I had come. My heart dropped as I considered what it would mean for these girls to have crayons or papers in a supply cabinet. Even a desk to write on would have been so beneficial to them. I thought about Hellen Keller and the formidable odds she overcame during her lifetime.

I gathered my thoughts and recalled all the girls with bicycles I had painted over the last year. I considered how independence and empowerment could be derived from something as simple, but complex, as an education. I thought about how receiving an education for these girls was not a simple thing at all. I imagined them walking miles to this schoolhouse every day in hopes of a brighter future.

Families from all around the village traveled several hours behind bull-pulled carts to see their daughters receive a bicycle at the ceremony. Everyone was asked to be seated, and I was escorted to my center place at the table. I scanned the room of faces while looking into the eyes of the parents and girls that were staring back at me. I realized how small I felt, how insignificant. I considered the enormous impact a bike would potentially have on their lives and how little I'd done in the last year to *really* make a difference. I was humbled at the thought of them taking time to listen to me speak. I felt shameful that I had been given so much in my life and taken my education for granted for so long. I was determined at that point to help these girls understand that their fight for an education was worth their efforts.

An interpreter was there to translate my speech. I began with how inspiring they were to me and how thankful and humbled I was to be able to see their school and meet them in person. I talked about the importance of fighting for an education and the rewards that could come from being a lifetime learner in order to fulfill their dreams. I told them they were all smart, brave and determined and these were three things they needed to continue to remind themselves of every single day. I gave them all 3" x 5" colored postcard prints with images I had painted over the course of the year. The cards had my mantra in both English and Khmer: *I am brave, I am smart, I am determined.*

The bike ceremony was something other-worldly. The girls were called up, one by one. They received a certificate, a bicycle, and a bike pump. It was explained to them that they had been selected because they had shown an overwhelming desire to learn. Both the girls and their families decided that education was critical and worth the additional work that it took to make it possible. They rightly earned these bicycles, and now they would enter into a program with Lotus Petals that would last for two years. These girls would be monitored by the organization and encouraged to continue their education. The bicycle became their promise to continue moving forward — a pact of sorts. It was as if they were all now part of a secret bike club.

Me at the bicycle ceremony in Siem Reap

Chapter 31
TAKE FLIGHT

*"You can't go back and change the beginning,
but you can start where you are and
change the ending."*
- C. S. Lewis

At a recent Horticultural Symposium that I attended with my mother, I was fascinated to learn that the design concepts of a garden are very similar to that of a painting: movement, shapes, vertical interest, focal points, and containers. I decided that it would be in my best interest to begin looking at my paintings as if I were planting a garden. The older I get, the more I realize and notice the overlapping nature of seemingly unrelated subjects. As a lifetime learner, I continue to make mistakes, research and learn. As my perspective shifts, I begin to see things in a different light.

A mosaic of events makes up all of our lives. Linking these events together to see the meaning and purpose is the real challenge. Finding purpose was my personal challenge. The passion was easy. We are all born with a passion. A passion to heal, a passion to teach, a passion to take care of others, a passion to lead, a passion to cook, a passion to dance, a passion to athletically compete or perhaps, a passion to garden. Everyone has a passion for something. Purpose, however, forces us to find direction.

The monarch butterfly's purpose is to migrate up to 2500 miles from North America to the same trees as their ancestors in remote parts of Mexico. Like that of the migrating monarch, once our purpose is defined, we begin to see clearly. Our eyes are open to new possibilities, and we believe in ourselves without fear of failure. Failure is something that is inevitable, but, with a defined purpose in place, failure can become an opportunity to learn and improve ourselves by opening up new and previously hidden pathways to success.

As painful as it may seem, there are many

benefits of failure. After a certain number of fail⸤ whether self-induced or out of our control, we beg⸜ to take greater risks. Not risks that will hurt us, but rather, risks that allow us to put ourselves out there for the possibility of success. Without fear of failure, we can finally reach our true potential. The realization that failure will not kill us is the secret to success. The fact that I have failed many times gives me prodigious strength to persevere and push at a different rate. It is entirely possible I am partially trying to prove to my parents that I am not a failure, though I am much more motivated by the idea of living a life infused with purpose and passion in service of others.

This brings me back to parenthood. Allowing my children to fail, may possibly be the most difficult thing that I will have to do as a mother. Watching my children make mistakes, and suppressing my instinct to help them, will enable them to become a better version of myself. Relinquishing complete control, after I've done all that seems age appropriate for them, will allow requisite room for growth and ultimate development — mistakes and all.

While in Cambodia, I learned the story of the lotus flower. The flower begins its life at the bottom of a muddy, dark, lifeless swamp-like environment. As the flower slowly rises above the murky waters, its pure, vibrant petals emerge unscathed. As their pedals reach towards the sky like a sun salutation they again, each night, retreat into the muddy waters. Their stems bend in every which way but are almost impossible to break by hand. They remain sturdy and stable in their unfavorable environment, regardless of their surroundings. In other words, oftentimes it is the hardships that make us stronger. Those that can continue to pull themselves up by their bootstraps, regardless of intermittent failings, often resist ultimate failure.

Our journey then, as parents of creative children, is to carefully guide them towards transforming their passion into something greater. Once passion turns to purpose, we can begin to see longer strides of success patterns. Looking at our child's life, as an outsider, can sometimes be both excruciating and frightening. Trust in time. From my experience, this path was not a linear one. The continued guidance and redirection of my parents eventually lead me towards a purposeful life. My passion for painting led me to find my purpose in helping others who are less fortunate than myself.

We moved nearly two years ago to a small town just north of Charlotte. I now work from my home studio which allows me to balance my life as well as my large-scale art projects. Just a few months ago, I successfully installed two separate, fourteen foot, triptych, mixed-media pieces into the Greenville-Spartanburg International Airport. Each painting individually spans over ten-thousand square inches across two separate airport walls. Both contemporary pieces depicts women on bicycles. Once again, I partnered with Lotus Pedals and donated a percentage of my sales to provide bicycles to young, underprivileged girls in Cambodia.

When my days come to an end, I do not wish to be known solely as a visual artist. I want to be remembered as an artist with a humanitarian drive that felt a visceral connection to give back through

Greenville-Spartanburg International Airport

her passion. If I could do it all over again, there are a lot of things I wouldn't necessarily choose for myself. But, because I cannot do this life all over again, there is nothing I would change. It took conflict to get to my calling. I am embracing my choices with the hope of allowing my children to break free from my mistakes. If it takes my own mistakes to help my children, or someone else's child, to repurpose their priorities, then my journey was worth it.

My education continues. As a forty-six-year-old married woman with two children, I am a self-proclaimed lifelong learner. I strive to look with compassion at my children as they succeed and fail, but with an invisible hand that helps to guide them towards their higher purpose. Because, in the end, it does not come down to where you graduated or your final GPA. It does not make a difference whether you have the newest leather pumps or silver bells dangling from your orthopedic shoes. It comes down to hard work, perseverance, strength of character, and resilience.

For me, my circuitous path resulted in combining passion with purpose in service of others. We *all* have a story to tell, and we all took our own distinct paths to get to where we are today. Life and success is a reflection of our ability to stand up and run again after we fall. Falling allows us to redirect our thinking and refocus our mission. After all, sometimes it is much easier to find perspective from sitting on the ground.

ACKNOWLEDGMENTS

The following people were invaluable in helping me through this educational and time-consuming journey:

To my parents, both of you continue to inspire me to be a better person. Thank you for never giving up on me.

To my son, James, for being the foundational inspiration of this book. Thank you for letting me tell my story and allowing me to compare myself to you. You have a huge head-start in life, simply by learning from all of my ridiculous mistakes. I am so proud of you, your hard work, and perseverance in school. I am excited to see your wonderful life unfold. You will go far, my love, I have no doubt in my mind.

To my daughter, Claudia, for listening to me read stories and passages of my life, for giving me sage advice, and for pretending to find it all fascinating.

To my husband, Walter, for being my quiet supporter and for the many ways you offered your editorial assistance in the final stages of the book. I appreciate you giving me affirmation along the way when I wanted to just tuck it all under the bed for no one to ever read. Thank you for encouraging me to make it to the finish line with this compilation of stories.

To my sisters, Kathryn and Glenn, thank you for being my life-long best friends — for this, I am eternally blessed and grateful.

And finally, to James T. Joyce, my father-in-law, a published author, columnist, editor and good friend. Thank you for being my first reader and editor. You made it all feel official.

ABOUT THE AUTHOR

Nancy Hilliard Joyce was born in Greenville, South Carolina. At the age of sixteen, she was accepted into the Governor's School for the Arts. For five years, she served on the Board of Trustees at the Asheville Art Museum and was an active member of the River Arts District Association in Asheville, NC. Today, Nancy is a board member of The Governor's School for the Arts Foundation, located in Greenville, South Carolina as well as The Cabarrus Arts Council Board located in Concord, North Carolina. She is the Art Curator for multiple boutique hotels and she regularly produces large-scale commission work. Nancy is passionate about giving back to the environment, women, and children in need and uses her art as a platform to raise money for charity and non-profit organizations.

Nancy's paintings are intricate in form and filled with layers of color, perspective, gestures, and expression. Her contemporary, mixed-media art is often created with modeling paste, a range of synthetic polymer paints, various handmade papers and detailed with touches of oil paint. She will sometimes sand or wipe down layers to reveal underlayers while building up other sections to create texture and depth; a process that may go on for weeks or end in just a day. Nancy's work is appreciated and widely collected throughout the United States in many homes, hotels, corporate offices, and airports. She is known as a contemporary, mixed- media artist with an Americana flair.

To view or collect Nancy's artwork, visit her website at NancyJoyceGallery.com or follow her page on Instagram or Facebook @NancyJoyceArt.

27230586R00131

Made in the USA
Columbia, SC
20 September 2018